The Farewell Christmas

WILLIAM S. SHIELDS

Tate Publishing & *Enterprises*

Published by Tate Publishing & Enterprises, LLC
127 E. Trade Center Terrace | Mustang, Oklahoma 73064 USA
1.888.361.9473 | www.tatepublishing.com

Tate Publishing is committed to excellence in the publishing industry. The company reflects the philosophy established by the founders, based on Psalm 68:11,
"The Lord gave the word and great was the company of those who published it."

Cover design by Anna Lee
Interior design by Christina Hicks

Published in the United States of America

ISBN: 978-1-61777-533-8
1. Biography & Autobiography / Personal Memoirs
2. Biography & Autobiogrpahy / General
11.04.07

Dedication

To my darling wife, Maria, you have been with me through thick and thin. If not for you I would not have been able to survive. You have always been, and always will be my true love and inspiration. You are a very good listener and an enthusiastic encourager. I know that you have heard all of my stories a million times, yet you always seem to smile when I tell them. Thank you for being such a wonderful friend and lover!

To the Shields family; my children, Kim, Billy, and Tom; my grandson, Alex; and the better halves, Victor, Sarah, and Lauren, I am truly blessed to have all of you in my life. Thank you to my sisters Ellen and Gloria and to my brother Tony. Dad was right when he said "without family you have nothing." I am very fortunate to have received the gift of a loving and supportive family that knows how to laugh and enjoy life.

My mother, Anna, my father, John, Grammy and Grandpa, Aunty Sue and Aunty Laura, thank you for watching over me. I know that all of you are looking down from that big supper table in God's kitchen and smiling. I'm sure Ma will say, "See, Billy turned out okay."

Yes, Ma, I have made it, thanks to the love and guidance that all of you gave to me, when we shared our love and passion for each other during the many feasts that we all enjoyed together.

To my big brother Jackie, thank you for always being there for me. I know that God took you to heaven because he needed someone strong and smart to help him with his duties. The life and legacy of Lieutenant John A. Shields will live forever in the pages of this book.

Table of Contents

Introduction

As time goes by in our lives and we have gone through the many trials and tribulations that take place between being a child and becoming a senior citizen, we have a tendency to reflect upon the positive experiences that we have lived through.

When I was a child of ten years old, I had the most memorable experience of spending Christmas with my family.

Although it was many years ago, I still remember that time in my life as if it were yesterday.

I have pondered and reflected upon this time in my life for several years. I have told the stories that took place back then many times and to numerous people. Several people suggested that I should consider writing a book about what took place back in 1956.

Writing a book has been a goal of mine for more years than I care to admit. But raising children and building a career kept me preoccupied with more important issues. There were many excuses but no practical reason why I could not accomplish my goal of sharing my story with the world.

When procrastination evaporates and motivation strikes, the transition is subtle. There are no bells ringing or light bulbs flashing; it just happens.

It was early December, and it had snowed the night before. I arrived at my office in the morning, and I sat down at my desk. I peered out my window and looked upon the fresh coating of snow that covered the roof of the adjacent building. Seeing the fresh snow on the rooftop and the bare limbs of the maple trees outside my window allowed my mind to wander back to Christmas in 1956.

I checked my messages, and then, after taking the lid off of my container of coffee, I punched up a blank page on my computer screen and typed "The Farewell Christmas: A Memoir by William S. Shields."

I began to put my memories in written form. Perhaps it was divine intervention or just a burning desire to tell a story that needs to be told, but I acquired the inspiration that I needed to finally tell my story.

Everyone has a story to tell; we just need some encouragement to tell it. I have been a storyteller just about my whole life. Now I have a chance to share my story with many others.

When we are young and impressionable we look at the world and never believe that it will change. We cherish the moments that we spend with our loved ones and never think that they will leave us. Innocence is blind to the happenings of life.

The story that you are about to read is a nostalgic tale of happiness and compassion. You will read about a family that enjoyed life as much as they enjoyed one another.

Anyone who has ever loved or has ever dreamed, no matter what age they are, will understand why love never dies.

Christmas in 1956 was a magical time for Billy Shields. Come and share my memories and find out why my book is titled The Farewell Christmas.

Anticipation

I woke up and started to get out of bed and then I realized this was going to be a very special day, a day that the Shields family had been anticipating for some time. It was December twenty-first, the day that my big brother Jackie was coming home for Christmas.

I quickly headed to the bathroom and brushed my teeth and got washed up and ready to face the day. As I was getting dressed I couldn't help but think of all the wonderful things that Jackie had accomplished and how exciting it would be to have him home again. Everyone seemed much happier when Jackie was around. Having their first born, number one son home from the navy sure did put a twinkle in my Mother's and Father's eyes. I finished getting dressed and hustled downstairs to join the family for breakfast. I entered the kitchen and said good morning to everyone. I sat down and took a sip from the glass of milk that Ma had put in front of me.

The only one not at the table yet was my brother Tony. Just as I took a sip of milk, Tony ambled into the kitchen. His big blue eyes sparkled with mischief. "Hey, sport," he said, "you got milk on your mustache."

I quickly wiped my forearm against my mouth and gave him a glare. Tony laughed. A strand of his light brown hair flicked in his eyes. Like my sister Gloria, he had a tendency to tease me.

As I was about to eat breakfast with my family, I could tell just by the atmosphere that everyone was very excited that Jackie was coming home later this afternoon.

Ma had kind of a dance step going as she bounced around the kitchen while she was making us tomato and eggs for breakfast. Dad was unusually chatty. He was talking to Tony about the upcoming basketball games he would be playing on the freshman team at Winchester High School. Dad, most of the time, would just sit at the head of the kitchen table and read the newspaper while he listened to the news on the radio. It was odd to see my father so engaging this morning.

Now that we were all at the breakfast table, Ma served the tomato and eggs in a big plate that she put in the middle of the kitchen table. She also set a plate of English muffins on the table. The plate of red tomatoes and yellow eggs sprinkled with green basil looked kind of Christmassy this morning.

As we ate our breakfast, Ellen eagerly asked Ma, "Did you talk to Jackie last night on the phone? What time did he say he would be home?"

Ma set her coffee cup on the kitchen table and looked at Ellen with a sparkle in her brown eyes. "Yes, I did talk to him. He said he would be spending the night in Philadelphia at his college classmate's apartment. He'll be getting on the road around eight a.m., which should put him in Winchester between five and six o'clock this afternoon." As she buttered an English muffin, she added, "Of course that depends on the traffic."

Tony, with a big smile on his face, said matter-of-factly, "Jackie is a jet pilot. He likes to go fast. He'll probably be home at noontime."

We all got a good laugh out of that one, except Ma, who frowned and said, "I hope he doesn't drive too fast."

Ellen was happy to hear that Jackie would soon be home. My sister Ellen was a year and a half younger than Jackie and worked in Boston for the New England Telephone Company. This morning she was wearing a Christmas sweater that Aunty Sue had knitted for her. The sweater was bright red with a green Christmas tree in the front. It looked very festive and good on Ellen. She was tall and thin with dark brown hair. The skirt that Ellen had on was black, which made the red really stand out. Ellen was excited that the people she worked with at the telephone company where going out for a Christmas lunch today at the Union Oyster House, which was right around the corner from her office on Bowdoin Street.

Ellen was like a second mother to me. She took me lots of places and was always buying me gifts. Ellen did lots of work around the house as well. With my mother working full time everyone needed to help out.

Gloria was my other sister. She was sixteen years old and a junior at Winchester High School. Gloria was talking with Ellen about her Christmas party at work today. While she was talking with Ellen, I got up from the table, and she made it a point to rub my head as I walked by her just so she could mess up my hair. Gloria sure could be a pest at times.

Gloria was born just as the Second World War began. She worked after school at the Winchester Hospital. Although always busy talking on the telephone or doing homework, she helped Ma by starting dinner and getting things ready before Ma got home from work.

Gloria was always a great sister, even though she teased me sometimes. From what I heard from Gloria's friends, I wasn't the only one she teased. Gloria was really pretty with bright blue eyes and a perky smile. Her hair was light brown, and she had the whitest teeth I had ever seen on anyone. She said that her Ipana toothpaste made them sparkle. She was skinny like Ellen but not as tall. All the boys liked Gloria, but she didn't give them the time of day. I heard this from Shelly Isabella's little brother Domenic, my classmate.

Tony was born just as the Second World War was ending. He always kept an eye out for me. Tony played basketball and football with me, and he took me fishing with him all the time. Tony was a great brother, but like Gloria, he had a tendency to tease me. We are a very loving family and a very teasing family as well. Tony was kind of tall compared to most of his friends. He had light brown hair and blue eyes. He had blond hair when he was little, but his hair got darker over the years.

As we finished breakfast, Ma reminded us that tonight was the Lincoln School Christmas pageant and that everyone had to go to see Billy perform in the big show. Ma had a smile on her face as she told us about the pageant. Ma had an attractive smile and a pretty face. She had turned fifty a couple of years ago and kiddingly complained that she was getting old all the time. She was actually in pretty good shape for someone in her fifties. She walked back and forth to work every day and scurried around the house like she was sprinting up heartbreak hill in the Boston Marathon. She was short, only five foot two, her hair was turning grey, and she wore glasses, but to me she was the sweetest and prettiest mother our Lord ever put on this earth.

Dad had gone to the back hall to get his coat and then came back and said good-bye to everyone as he kissed Ma on his way out the door. Dad was a stocky guy with large shoulders and big arms. He had gotten a little heavier since he quit smoking a year or so ago.

He had a full head of grayish brown hair that he combed back like Humphrey Bogart, giving him a very distinguished look. Like my mother, he wore eye glasses. During the Second World War Dad had an accident while he was in the Aleutian Islands. He was working with an army transport construction crew, and as they were hoisting cargo from a transport ship, the shackle that was holding the load broke and a piece of the metal shackle split off and hit my father in the mouth, cracking one of his front teeth. The tooth was chipped and discolored to a light shade of tan that when he smiled made him look roguish.

Everyone was off to school or work. When we convened for supper that night, we would have the whole family together for the first time in a long time.

The Paper Route

I had to stay after school and clean the erasers that afternoon. What a pain in the neck. With the extra time I had to spend at school, I would just make it to the news store in time to pick up the two-wheel dolly and hightail it down to the train station by 3:45.

As I walked to the back of the news store to pick up the two-wheel dolly, I could feel the bitter wind whipping through the alley. I gripped my coat collar close to my neck and hurried toward the train station to collect the five-star late edition of the Boston Record American. On that first day of winter, the nearly abandoned streets of Winchester, Massachusetts, seemed dreary under the cloudy gray sky. The sign on the National Bank building flashed seventeen degrees. I couldn't believe that, only a couple of weeks ago when I attended the Thanksgiving Day football game between Winchester and Woburn, the sign flashed fifty degrees.

As I passed the front of the news store, Charlie Vassali, the biggest mouth and toughest bully of all the paperboys, popped out of the door. His thick brows and dark scowl made shivers run through my skinny, ten-year-old body. "Hey, Shields, you better get your ass up to the train station. It's Christmas week. We don't want to piss the customers off by delivering the newspaper to them late. After all, this is the week us paperboys wait for all year. We finally get our Christmas tips from those cheap bastard customers on our paper routes."

Although I was already on my way to the station, I didn't want to give Charlie any back talk. He was a Saint Mary's School kid. It seemed that the kids that went to sister school always had the biggest trash mouths.

As the youngest in Mr. Mullen's stable of paperboys, I had the dubious job of waiting for the train and bringing the late edition of the Record American to the news store so that the paperboys could deliver them along with the Boston Globe, The Boston Traveler, and The Christian Science Monitor.

The train was late as usual. I would have to hustle through my paper route if I was going to be on time for the Lincoln School Christmas Pageant at 7:30 p.m. It wasn't like I had a great part in the pageant or anything. Jack Fogerty was playing Joseph again and Jane Finch was playing Mary. I was banished to the choir. I'm sure it was because of my great singing voice!

Besides tonight being the big Christmas Pageant, by the time I finished my paper route, my brother Jackie would be home from Florida for his Christmas vacation. He was stationed in Pensacola, Florida. Jackie was a fighter pilot. Actually Jackie had been flying in air shows with the Blue Angels. The Blue Angels are the navy's precision flying team. The Blue Angels fly in formation and do all sorts of stunts and tricks with their jets while they are flying at close to five hundred miles per hour.

My brother Jackie was one of the youngest pilots ever to fly with a navy air show team. Jackie had always been gifted. He got two double promotions while he was in the Winchester school system. He graduated high school when he was sixteen years old and got his bachelor of science degree from college on the day he turned twenty.

Jackie was an exceptional student and was still showing his educational skills. He had mastered the skill of flying jet airplanes. I can only imagine what you have to study and learn to be able to understand the workings of an aircraft that can fly faster than the speed of sound.

Jackie had been away since last Christmas. It was always a big deal when he came home for the holidays. Jackie was the oldest child in our family. There were five children in the Shields family. I was the youngest at ten years old. Jackie was twenty-three and had already earned the rank of lieutenant in the United States Navy. I had just recently stopped sleeping with stuffed animals. I guess there was quite a maturity swing in the age range and accomplishments in the Shields brood.

Jackie had the look of a Saturday matinee movie star. With his dark complexion and strong chin, coupled with his dark hair and infectious smile, standing six feet tall, this guy looked like what a fighter pilot should look like.

Not only was the return of Lieutenant John A. Shields a big deal to me, it was a big deal to everyone in our community. Jackie had become a hero to our small town just north of Boston.

The local newspaper was always printing something about Jackie's accomplishments. Just last month there was an article in the newspaper about Jackie breaking the sound barrier in his F7U Cutlass jet. They had a picture of Jackie receiving a replica of the plane and a commendation from the plane's manufacturer, Chance-Vought Aircraft Company.

In addition to his accomplishments as a fighter pilot, Jackie had a history of, well, just being a good person. One example of his gallantry would be when Jackie was working for the Town of Winchester Water Department as a summer job a few years ago.

While he was working there was a pretty big brush fire up by the town reservoir. The foreman of the crew, Mr. Carter, was riding the fire line when his truck got stuck right in the path of the runaway brush fire. The story goes that Mr. Carter was trapped along with his truck, and that if my brother Jackie had not come along and helped him get his truck moving and escape the area, Mr. Carter and his truck might not have made it out of the fire. Jackie got some kind of commendation for that act of heroism.

In his freshman year, Jackie, only thirteen, received a varsity letter in cross country. He must have been a pretty darn good runner to have accomplished the task of receiving a varsity letter at such a young age. Then again, if I had Charlie Vassali chasing me, I might have been able to break a world speed record myself.

As for local heroes, I would have to say that along with Jackie, all of my brothers and sisters were heroes to me as well. As I said, I was the youngest of five, and it's no secret that I got into all sorts of mischief. Thank God my brothers and sisters were looking after me and kept me out of the line of fire from parents, teachers, and just about everyone else that would have liked to get a paddle on my skinny little butt!

The five Shields children, along with our parents, Annie and John, just loved being together and sharing stories and accounts of our day when we sat down for supper. Tonight would be a very special night because Jackie was scheduled to arrive home just around supper time. I had a feeling that this Christmas was going to be a very special one.

Finally, at long last, the 3:45 train came chugging down the tracks. Mr. Bagely, the conductor, was hanging out of the door of the train as it made its way from Wedgemere Station to the center of town. Mr. Bagely was a nice man; he always helped me put the newspapers on the two-wheel dolly. He really did look like a railroad train conductor because he wore the blue uniform and the conductor's hat with the gold B&M symbol in the center of his cap. He was average in height and just a little stocky. He had rosy cheeks (mostly from the cold weather I think), and he had a gray mustache that sat just above his upper lip. He also had that air of authority that a train conductor should have.

As I was the smallest of the paperboys and had to muscle the bundles of papers onto to the two-wheel dolly every afternoon, I was always thankful that Mr. Bagely gave me a hand putting the papers on the dolly.

I took the paper route over from my brother Tony in the fall because he was going to be playing basketball and could not do the route anymore. I really didn't mind doing the paper route. It was nice having the money, and this week was the big pay off!

As the train slowly rolled down the tracks toward the train station, I couldn't help but admire how bright and shiny the new Boston & Maine Railroad Budliner cars were. It had only been about a year or so since the Boston & Maine Railroad switched from coal to diesel on the locomotive engines. At the same time, they had eliminated the old Pullman cars and added the Budliner stainless steel passenger cars. On the front of each Budliner car sat a big blue "B" with a white "M" crossing the middle of the "B" on the front of each Budliner car. They really did look cool.

About the same time that the Boston & Maine railroad switched from coal to diesel, they completed the elevation of the railroad tracks through Winchester. A couple of years before, the trains ran at street level, and when a train came through Winchester Center they had to put the crossing gates down and stop all the traffic. With more automobiles on the road since the end of the Second World War and there being so many trains coming through town, the railroad thought it would be safer if they elevated the tracks and put bridges through town for the trains to go over rather than stopping the traffic on the streets.

The railroad station was brand-new and was made of fancy stone and concrete. The ramps that went up to the inbound and outbound tracks were paved. They had a green railing sitting on top of a granite curb that made the new train station look really smart.

"Hi, Billy, how are you this afternoon?" Mr. Bagely shouted as the train pulled into the station.

"I'm doing just fine, Mr. Bagely," I yelled back. Mr. Bagely was hard of hearing from all the years he had spent riding on the noisy trains. I doubt very much if Mr. Bagely ever heard my reply to his standard greeting every day.

"Here is the late edition of the Record American," Mr. Bagely mumbled as he threw the first bundle of newspapers down while lowering the stair ramp for the passengers to get off. He helped me put the bundles of papers on the two-wheel dolly. "It's cold as a witch's tit today, huh, Billy?"

"It sure is, Mr. Bagely," I replied. I was a little taken aback at Mr. Bagely's comment to me because he was always so professional in all of his duties.

Hearing a grown man, and a professional person at that, saying a swear word kind of surprised me. I know that grown-ups swear a lot, but swears are seldom said in my house. My mother lets out a few choice words every once in a while, but she always says her swears in Italian.

I moved down the ramp from the train station as fast as I could with the two-wheel dolly. As I turned the corner from the ramp to Waterfield Street I almost knocked a little old lady over. I apologized to her, but she was in such a hurry with her head down and her scarf pulled around her face that she didn't pay any attention to me.

I pushed the dolly up Thompson Street and got the newspapers to the back of the news store so that Mr. Mullen could dole them out to the waiting paperboys. I got my papers and headed out to do my paper route.

The long walk up Shore Road was a killer. The wind was whipping across Judkin's Pond. It's always cold and windy walking up Shore Road. Shore Road is a desolate strip of land that runs parallel to the railroad tracks. Shore Road connects the Italian section of town, known as the Italian Village, to the center of town.

The walk up Shore Road was as dreadful as I had feared. With my bag of newspapers made heavier by all the extra Christmas advertising and the fierce, howling headwind, I felt like a drunken sailor trying to walk on board the deck of a ship during a hurricane.

I was about three quarters of the way up Shore Road, with Mrs. Napoli's house in sight. The Napoli's house is the first house on my paper route and was at the part of the road where Shore Road ended and turned into Spruce Street. This is a big green house with a barn off to the side. The Napolis, like most of the people in the village, had a garden and would use most of their land for growing vegetables. There was a small front walk and about five steps to their front door. I was always happy to climb those steps as it meant the end of my walk up that long, windy road.

All of a sudden I could hear a car pull up behind me. I moved to the side of the road to let the car go by. I kept trudging forward, but this car was still behind me. I turned around to look at the jerk that was almost running me over. As I looked over my right shoulder I saw a beautiful, brand-new Mercury Monterey. It was two-tone blue with skirts over the rear wheels. This was a real beauty! Then I noticed Florida license plates on the front of the car. All of a sudden the horned beeped and scared the life out of me. The car pulled up next to me and the power window rolled down. I looked through the window and just stood there staring for a moment. I'm sure I looked a little dumbfounded at this point because of who I saw driving the car.

All of a sudden I heard a voice that I had not heard for a very long time. "Hey kid, you got the Pensacola Gazette?"

As this state of affairs finally began to sink in, my eyes flew wide open, and I realized that it was my brother Jackie!

"Get in the car before you freeze to death," he yelled to me.

I was so happy to hear his voice and for him inviting me to get in the car. I opened the back door and put the bag of newspapers on the backseat. I then opened the front door and jumped in the car.

The Homecoming

"So how have you been? I've missed you," Jackie said. "Everything going okay with you? Hey, no one knows I'm home yet; Ma doesn't expect me for another hour. I'll drive you around to do the paper route; how does that sound? I bet that I can still remember who gets what paper. Did Tony tell you who the good tippers are? This paper route has been in the family since 1944. I delivered both of the newspapers that announced VE Day and VJ Day. I'll never forget both of those days. How is Tony doing on the freshman basketball team?"

I sat frozen in place, still startled by his sudden appearance, yet so happy to see and listen to him. I stared back with what must have looked like a dumb expression.

Apparently I was not answering his questions fast enough because he blurted out, "Hey, what's the matter with you? Cat got your tongue or something?"

Ah, the ever-loving taunt of my older brother. Although he is the older brother and the respected returning hero, he is no different from the rest of my siblings. Giving each other a playful insult is part of our nature, I guess.

I finally came back to reality, and I got my senses back. I told Jackie, "Tony was doing well on the basketball team, and I learned who the good tippers were all by myself."

With the unexpected arrival of Jackie I'm sure I was looking pretty stupid to my customers as they came to the door to get the newspaper and saw me with this big huge smile on my face looking as if I'd just won the Irish Sweepstakes.

Having Jackie home and having him all to myself was a pretty big deal. I loved him very much, and I really missed having him home. It was always special when we had the whole family together, all of us sitting around the supper table and sharing what was going on in our lives.

When we're are all together and sharing conversation and giving one another a little taunt or dig, I sometimes watch both of my parents as they smile and have this look of being proud parents on their faces. Sharing our thoughts and love for one another, and yes, a choice barb or two, was something special, and it would be extra special now that Jackie had come home.

We moved through the first part of the paper route quickly. Jackie would hand me the newspaper when I come back to the car as I ran back and forth from house to house. He was right; he did remember who took what newspaper. I was impressed that after all those years he still knew who takes what newspaper.

As we got to the end of Swanton Street Jackie let me know, "I'm going to take a quick run into Neno's Market to say hello to Gladys and Neno Marcheese."

Jackie worked for them at the grocery store when he was in high school. He would tell me stories about how he had to hitch up Speedy the horse to the wagon that Neno would drive throughout the village selling fruits and vegetables to the neighbors. Even though Neno had the store he would still peddle his goods door-to-door to those that could not make it to the grocery store. Speedy the horse died a couple of years after Jackie worked at the store. Neno then purchased an old bus that he drove around the neighborhood peddling his fruits and vegetables.

Jackie always had an excellent sense of respect for just about everyone that he came in contact with. Stopping by to visit with Neno and Gladys was something that he felt was important.

Neno's Market, as the sign said outside over the door, was the biggest of the stores in the neighborhood. They had a full-sized store that was a brick building with big glass windows in the front. Unlike the other little corner stores in the village, Neno's had an aisle for fruits and vegetables and a few aisles with canned goods and macaroni and stuff. They had a meat market in the back of the store with glass cases filled with steaks and other kinds of roasts and meats. Next to the meat cases was the cold cut case where they have the salami and capicola and lots of cheeses.

Neno's was the biggest grocery store in the neighborhood, but it was not quite as big as the First National Store in Winchester center.

Jackie walked into the store and immediately he got a big smile and a warm reception from Neno and Gladys. I stood next to him as he answered all of their questions. Jackie seemed to bring a smile to every face that he came in contact with. Neno and Gladys were very interested in how it was for him to be flying jet airplanes. Jackie being a naval aviator was something that the people in our neighborhood found most intriguing. Many of the first generation immigrants in the village lost a son or a brother or an uncle or some family relation to the war in Europe and Japan. Having Jackie Shields as a fighter pilot and an officer in the United States Navy gave everyone in the village a better feeling about our country.

As we got back in the car I told Jackie, "Tonight is the Lincoln School Christmas Pageant."

Jackie said, "I'm thrilled to know that I made it home in time to attend the big event." Then he asked me, "Is Mr. Benson still the janitor at the Lincoln School?"

"He's still the janitor," I told him. "He asks me how you're doing all the time."

Jackie explained, "Mr. Benson was always good to me. I'll always have a special spot in my heart for Mr. Benson. I was new to the school, and he made it a point to see that I found my way around okay."

The Lincoln School Christmas pageant gave the kids a chance to be in the spotlight and gave the parents and relatives the opportunity to be proud of their children.

This was a humble neighborhood made up of hard-working people that seldom got the occasion to be full of pride. The Christmas pageant, no matter how goofy it seemed (especially to me), was no doubt an important annual event in our little corner of the world.

We finished the paper route in record time. It was the first time I had ever been driven around to deliver my papers. The last paper that we delivered was right next to Amos Napoli's barber shop and pool hall.

Jackie said to me, "I'm going to stop in and say hello to Amos and the guys in the pool hall; you wait for me here in the car."

Amos Napoli is the brother-in-law of Mrs. Napoli, the first customer on my paper route. Many of the people in the village are related and lots of the last names are the same.

The pool hall was a gathering and gambling spot for many of the guys in the neighborhood. Jackie admits to spending a few idle afternoons at Amos Napoli's pool hall.

When I got a haircut at Amos's barbershop, I always looked back in the pool room to see what it looked like. It had a big pool table in the middle with one light hanging from the ceiling directly over the middle of the pool table. There were no windows, so it was very dark except for the pool table itself, which was illuminated by the one florescent light. It looked kind of spooky because the light was so bright and right under the hanging light you saw waves of smoke drift across the pool table. I guess playing pool and smoking go hand in hand.

There were also signs on the wall that always amused me. They said, "If you can't pay, don't play," "No spitting," "Be respectful to one another," and my favorite, "No Gambling."

Jackie gave a quick hello to Amos and then checked the backroom to say hello to the guys. There were a few of the younger guys and one or two of the guys that Jackie grew up with. The guys were happy to see Jackie. They all gave him a handshake and asked him when he got home and how long he would be home for. Jackie made a little small talk and then said goodbye to everyone.

Before we headed for home Jackie decided to treat me to a Hires Root Beer at Mrs. Mele's corner store. While we were sitting on the stools, drinking our root beer, who shuffled through the door but Adagio. He was one of the many characters that we had in the neighborhood. Adagio was the son of the local "Don," and he had Parkinson's disease. The disease made his hand shake and he dragged his leg and slurred his words. He was a nice old guy but just a little "shaky" as the kids called him. Jackie gave me a wink as he said, "Hello, Adagio; how have you been?"

You could tell that Adagio was happy to see Jackie. He had a big smile on his face as he put out is quivering hand for Jackie to shake.

Jackie gladly shook hands with Adagio. As he shook his hand, Jackie patted him on the shoulder and looked him in the eyes as he said, "It's good to see you again, Adagio."

Adagio mumbled to Jackie, "The other day, when I was walking downtown, I saw you in your jet plane fly over my head in the sky."

Jackie told Adagio, "The next time you see me fly over head you should wave to me."

"I'll make sure that I wave the next time I see you fly over Winchester."

Adagio shuffled off with a grin on his face and said, "Good-bye."

Jackie turned to me with a big smile and said, "I'm stationed in Pensacola, Florida. I would probably have to refuel twice to make it up to Winchester from there. But if Adagio believes he saw me flying over Winchester, then good for him. I'm not going to burst his bubble."

We got back in the car and headed down Swanton Street, and then turn onto Spruce Street. As we made the turn on to Spruce Street, Jackie said, "Let's stop by and say a quick hello to Grandpa before we go home. I want to let him know I made it home safely."

I told Jackie, "That sounds like a good idea to me."

Jackie figured he will say a quick hello to Grandpa and then say hello to Aunty Sue and Aunty Laura that night at the school pageant. Jackie thought it better to catch Grandpa before the aunts got home from their jobs at the Schraft's candy factory in Charlestown. Grandpa had sugar diabetes and had his left leg removed from just above the knee a couple of years ago. He had to wear a wooden leg. Because of his wooden leg, Grandpa didn't make it to many functions unless they were at my house.

Like all of the Shields kids, Jackie had great love for Grandpa. Jackie understood that if it was not for Grandpa helping out with money for him to go to college that he might never have achieved his goal of becoming a jet pilot and flying with one of the most elite flying teams in the world.

We had a routine we went through when we walk through the front door at Grandpa's house. It started with "Come sta il Papa-Nona?" (How are you, Grandpa?), and we usually get the same reply every time from Grandpa: "Medza-Medz" (which means so-so).

Actually Jackie could speak Italian very well. Jackie was pretty good at conversing with Grandpa in his native language. Grandpa spoke very little English but knew enough to get by. As we walked through the door, Grandpa looked over from his easy chair and saw Jackie and me. Grandpa broke out in a big smile and began to clap his hands together in happiness as he saw Jackie enter the room. You could see a gleam in Grandpa's eyes as he greeted Jackie. "Buona sera, Jackie, come sei!" Grandpa sang out.

Jackie had always been very close with Grandpa and Grammy. As a matter of fact, Jackie was with my grandmother just before she died. Jackie spent a lot of time with Grammy and Grandpa growing up as a child and lived upstairs from them for many years. Jackie lived in the apartment upstairs while my father was away for three years during the Second World War. Jackie always enjoyed spending time with Grammy and Grandpa.

Jackie gave Grandpa a big hug and a kiss. You could see how happy Grandpa was to see Jackie. He had tears in his eyes as he hugged Jackie.

Jackie began to tell Grandpa all about his trip home from Florida and how it was to be in the navy and to fly jet airplanes. As Jackie chatted with Grandpa he puffed away on his Parodi stogie, stopping every few puffs to flick the ashes in the big ash tray next to his chair. Jackie told Grandpa how it was always sunny and warm in Florida. Grandpa told Jackie that it sounded like the weather in Florida was similar to the weather in Naples, Italy, where he grew up.

Grandpa motioned for me to come over to him. He gave me a kiss on the cheek, then, in his best broken English, told me, "Please get me and Jackie a glass of wine to toast Jackie's return."

I got them both a glass of wine. Grandpa, as he always did, offered me a sip of his wine. They continued to talk. Grandpa nodded his head a lot as Jackie talked, but I really don't think he understood much of what Jackie was telling him. Grandpa had a big smile on his face though, and you could tell that he was really happy to see Jackie and to have him home for the holidays.

Jackie and Grandpa finished their glass of wine. Jackie told Grandpa that it was time for us to leave, but he would see him tomorrow. Jackie gave Grandpa a hug and a kiss as I did, and we waved good-bye as we headed out to go home.

Ma got a ride home from Roy Horn, the owner of the laundry where she works. Ellen had just gotten home from her job in Boston at the telephone company. Dad was home from his job in the Boston Naval Shipyard, where he was a rigger in charge of hoisting cargo and parts onto the many ships located in the navy yard.

Gloria got home early from her job at the Winchester Hospital. The only one not home yet was Tony, who was still at basketball practice. At long last the long-awaited homecoming of Jackie was about to take place.

As we pulled into the driveway, Jackie, the prankster, turned to me and said, "How about we get a rise out of Ma?"

I asked him, "How are we going to do that?"

"When you get inside turn to Ma, and tell her that while you were doing your paper route you came across someone that looked like they could use a good home-cooked meal. You let Ma know that you brought the guy home with you and that he is waiting outside for you to go and get him. I'm sure that she will hem and haw but will say it's okay. You then open the back door, and I'll come walking in and surprise her."

My mother was a very generous and compassionate person. My telling her that I found someone that needs a good home-cooked meal would not be unusual for our family. At one time or another everyone in the family has brought someone home to share supper with our family. We have had more friends, neighbors, and relatives sit down for dinner with us than most homeless shelters. My mother had this thing about feeding people. She loved to say, "Sit down; eat with us; we have plenty."

With this thought in mind I figured that Jackie's little prank should work just fine. Sure enough, I walked through the door and saw everyone in our big kitchen. I got a warm greeting as I entered the room.

Ma was always happy to see any one of her children, she came over and gave me a big hug and a kiss and said, "You must be freezing from being out in the wind and cold all afternoon."

Dad asked, "Did you bring me home the late edition of The Record American?"

Gloria asked, "Is chicken bones ready for the big pageant tonight?" (Gloria thought I was skinny and had given me the nickname chicken bones.)

Ellen, who was always thinking of me, let me know, "I have a surprise for you, Billy." Ellen usually brought me home something special from Boston, a candy bar or a comic book.

I said hello to everyone, and then I dropped the bomb on Ma and said to her, "While I was doing my paper route this afternoon, I came across someone that looked like they could use one of your wonderful home-cooked meals. I told him that my mother always makes extra to eat and that one more mouth to feed at the supper table shouldn't be a problem."

Ma looked at me with a concerned expression on her face, and then after contemplating my request she said, "Oh well, I'm sure we can squeeze another in at the table for supper tonight."

I headed back toward the door and started to open it as if I was going to go get the hungry stranger when the door burst open and Jackie jumped through the door and into the kitchen!

Ma looked like she was going to have a heart attack. Ma dropped the bowl she was holding onto the counter and ran over and gave Jackie a big hug and a kiss. Ellen and Gloria were now standing right next to Ma as they wait their turn to give Jackie a welcome home hug and kiss. Dad got up from his spot where he was sitting at the head of the table and walked toward Jackie and held his hand out and gave Jackie a hearty handshake; then he grabbed Jackie and gave him a hug. Dad was not known for many outbursts of affection. I took the situation in and considered this show of emotion to be something special for Dad. I guess everyone really was excited to have Jackie home.

As everyone was hugging and kissing Jackie, the back door opened again, and in walked my brother Tony from basketball practice. Tony saw Jackie and ran over and gave him a big hug around the waist. Wow, what a welcome home!

The commotion died down and Mom let us know, "Supper will be ready in just a few minutes, so everyone should wash up and get ready to eat."

It was Wednesday night. This meant one thing: macaroni for supper. Ma always made macaroni on Wednesday nights. Ma used the leftover tomato sauce, meatballs, and sausages from Sunday's dinner for Wednesday night's supper. Along with the macaroni, meatballs, and sausages, Ma added a big tossed salad and a basket of fresh Italian bread from Marino's bakery.

We all assembled and took our designated places at the table, except for Ellen and Gloria, who were helping Ma put the food on the table. The way we scrambled to the table you would think that the attendant at the Stoneham Zoo was about to throw a raw steak in the lions' cage.

For the people that lived in the village this meal would be a standard Wednesday night dinner. However, it always seemed like a feast when Ma put her signature touch on the fixings. The bread was always fresh because we were lucky enough to live right next door to the Italian bakery. The aroma of the tomato sauce had a hint of garlic and basil. The meatballs were big and plump, as if they had just been picked from a meatball tree. The salad was a standard Italian salad, but the way that Ma mixed in the olive oil and wine vinegar dressing, you thought that a renowned chemistry professor from Harvard had concocted the blend.

The wine vinegar that Ma used was from Grandpa's annual wine-making endeavor. Each fall Grandpa made about four barrels of wine. (Yes, even with his wooden leg he still got involved with the wine making process; my father and us kids did most of the work. Grandpa just supervised.) Grandpa would take some of the wine and let it go bad, as he said. This is when you let the wine stay uncorked so it will turn to vinegar.

The olive oil Ma used for the salad dressing was Pastene, a standard brand used in most Italian households. There was nothing fancy or out of the ordinary in the way Ma makes the salad dressing. Nevertheless when Ma put things together they seemed to turn into a heavenly mixture. I think it might have been the amount of salt and pepper that she carefully applied to the top of the salad just before she tossed it.

We started with the macaroni. We were having mustacioli. I seemed to have this uncanny ability to remember every type of macaroni that the Prince Macaroni Company manufactured. I was not able to remember who wrote the Magna Carta or the Bill of Rights, but I sure did know my macaroni. I guess at ten years old I had certain priorities in life.

Ma always put the macaroni individually in each person's plate rather than serving the macaroni in a big bowl. We put our own tomato sauce on the macaroni, as each one of us seemed to like different amounts of sauce. The meatballs and sausages were in a big bowl and got passed around. We got to take as many as we liked.

As always, before we started to eat my dad would say grace. Dad said a special blessing because the eldest child had returned home and it was a special occasion.

Dad gave thanks by saying, "Jesus, thank you for Jackie's safe arrival home. We ask that the time we spend together as a family during this Christmas season be a very blessed time." He then continued by saying, "Bless us, oh Lord, for these thy gifts which we are about to receive from thy bounty through Christ our Lord, Amen."

We all chimed in at the same time with a loud amen.

We ate and talked; Jackie shared some of his experiences with us. We all had so many questions for him. Jackie was as patient as a watchmaker, the way he answered everyone's questions. Jackie seemed to glow as he let us share in his special world. Jackie was not pretentious or arrogant as he talked about aircraft carrier landings and making precision moves at four hundred miles an hour above the earth while he was making navigational calculations on a pad that was strapped to his right knee. It was a magical dinner that we all shared together.

We finished the main course. Ellen and Gloria cleared the dishes as Ma brought us Indian pudding for dessert to the table. Ma may have worked full time pressing shirts at the Embassy Laundry all day, but she still seemed to put together a great meal for us every evening. As Ma served the Indian pudding, Ellen put coffee cups on the table, and Gloria brought the fresh pot of coffee over. Coffee was always the finishing touch to our meals. The family took a few extra minutes to enjoy something sweet and sip Maxwell House coffee. Just like the commercial on the television show I Remember Mama, "Maxwell House Coffee was good to the last Drop!"

Getting Ready for the Big Event

Everyone helped clear the dishes from the table so that we could all get ready for the Christmas pageant. Even though all of my brothers and sisters were older, they still made a big deal out of the Lincoln School Christmas pageant. I guess it brought back memories for all of them.

Dad had to leave early to go to the school because he was the president of the Lincoln School Dad's Club. He had to help them get things ready in the school hall. My dad was always there to help in whatever way he could. Not only was he a physically strong man, he was also a very compelling man that would lend his support to whoever needed a hand.

The back doorbell rang. I answered the door and found my two best friends, Steve Maffeo and Bobby Melo. Steve and Bobby were in my class at school and were in the school pageant with me. Steve was lucky enough to have an actual part in the play; he was a shepherd boy. I'm not sure why he was picked to be a shepherd boy. Perhaps it was his puppy dog eyes and his small stature. Steve was a little smaller than the other kids in the class; he had a dark complexion, and his hair was charcoal black. He also had kind of a sullen look and did not show a lot of emotion in his demeanor. I guess those were important qualities if you were a shepherd boy.

Bobby, on the other hand, must have had a great voice, because he was in the choir with me. He was a happy-go-lucky kid that liked to joke around, almost the opposite of Steve. Bobby was always smiling; he had reddish-brown curly hair that when he let it grow out, he looked a little bit like Little Orphan Annie. He was kind of thickset but not chubby or anything like that. He had dark green eyes, and when he laughed real hard his face turned beet red. Steve and Bobby were really good friends.

"My dad is going to give us a ride to school," I told Steve and Bobby.

We waited for my dad on the back porch. The back porch was closed-in as of last summer. Dad made it like a three-season sunroom. The back porch did not have any heat, but it was an okay place to hang out and horse around for a few minutes.

Steve and Bobby were anxious to see Jackie. They had not seen Jackie since he was home last Christmas. Flying with the crack Navy precision flying team, the Blue Angels, had given him hero status in the Village.

I told Steve and Bobby, "Jackie is taking a shower and shaving. You guys will see him at the school in a little while."

Steve and Bobby were both very adamant about getting a glimpse of Jackie before we left for the pageant.

All of a sudden I got this brilliant idea. When Dad closed the back porch in, it made the bathroom window inside and it now looked out onto the closed-in back porch. Jackie was taking a shower right next to where we were playing. I decide to take a quick peek and see if he was still in the bathroom. Sure enough as I peeked through the bathroom window from the porch I could see that he was standing in front of the bathroom mirror with a towel around his waist, and his face was full of shaving cream.

Although the hot water from the shower had steamed up the window a little, you could still get a good look at him.

I told Steve and Bobby, "For you guys to get a look at the famous Navy fighter pilot shaving it will cost the both of you a dime each."

Without hesitation Steve and Bobby reached in their pockets and retrieve a shiny dime, and without any remorse I took the dime from each one of them. Ah, the benefits of having a celebrity in the family!

Steve and Bobby moved over to the window and got on their tiptoes and looked through the foggy glass and got their view of the famous fighter pilot. Both of them at the same moment let out a whispering sigh and said, "Cooool."

As I was putting the two dimes in my pocket, the back door opened, and my father came out. Dad asked, "You guys ready to go?"

I answered for all of us, "Yeah, Dad, we're all ready to go."

We headed out into the bone-chilling cold and quickly jumped into my dad's green Studebaker Hornet. It was a cool car for an old guy like my father. It was very basic but had style. Dad was a close to the belt kind of guy, no frills and nothing fancy. Dad was a true Scotsman and was very frugal. But the 1954 Studebaker was a sporty car with a front grill that had a big silver cone in the middle that looked a little like a torpedo sticking out of the grill, and the rear of the car was swept back and streamlined with fins.

Yes, that was right, my dad was a Scotsman, born in a suburb of Glasgow, Scotland (Bells Hill). My dad came to America when he was a child. His father had been a coal miner in Scotland, so when his family came to America they settled in Wilkes Barre, Pennsylvania, which is known for its coal mines.

Dad came east to the Boston area after graduating from high school. He had a tough upbringing as a kid. His mother passed away when he was young, and his father drank a lot and was very abusive, so Dad had to help the family out by going to school during the day and working at night.

We never really delved into my father's past. Anytime one of us asked Ma any questions about Dad's family, my mother would tell us, "Don't ask your father any questions about his family; he doesn't like to talk about his childhood."

Like the good children that we were, we just didn't ask him anything about his days growing up in Wilkes Barre, Pennsylvania.

When Dad came east, he rented a room in a boarding house in Newton Upper Falls, Massachusetts. It was during the Depression, and families took in boarders to get a little extra money. Dad lived with an Italian family that owned the house. This family had a son that was the same age as my dad. My father would eat meals with the family, and he became very friendly with their son. Dad was a quick learner, so he picked up the mannerisms and customs of this Italian family, and he also picked up some of the Italian language.

One Saturday night my father and the son of the people that owned the boarding house decided to go to a Sons of Italy dance in Medford, Massachusetts, which is the next town to Winchester. It just so happens that my mother and her sisters decided to go to the same Sons of Italy dance that night. The story goes that my father asked my mother to dance, and he became immediately infatuated with her. He dated her and spent quite a bit of time at my grandfather's house. It did not take long for my father to fall in love with my mother. This, however, posed a problem. During the time that my parents were dating my father passed himself off as being Italian. He actually used an alias, Johnny Nastro, during their courtship.

The predicament was that my father is Scottish and my mother is Italian. It was not really accepted back then that an Italian girl would marry someone that was not Italian. This was considered a mixed marriage. It became a real challenge for my father when he had to ask my grandfather for his daughter's hand in marriage.

Thank God my grandfather was so understanding and somewhat ahead of his time. When my father finally revealed to my grandfather that he was not Italian and that he wanted to marry his daughter, my grandfather, in his best broken English, said to my father, "John, you are a good man. You are very good to my daughter, and you make her happy. Of course you can marry my daughter."

My father has always been very thankful to my grandfather, and during his marriage to my mother he has gone out of his way to be good and helpful to Grandpa, especially during my grandfather's ordeal when he had his leg removed.

As a result of their mixed marriage the children of John and Anna Shields were now considered mongrels in the eyes of some of the old-fashioned Italians that live in the Village.

I remember the first time that I was called a mongrel. I ran home to ask my mother, "What is a mongrel?"

My mother asked me, "Why do you want to know?"

I told her, "Amos Napoli, the barber, said to the people in the barber shop when I came in, 'Here comes the little mongrel.'"

When I told her this she exclaimed, "That no good basta bastardo! Who does he thinks he is!"

Ma never really liked Amos Napoli anyway because of the pool hall and the gambling. This little episode about him calling me a mongrel was just the icing on the cake.

She told me, "The next time he calls you that you tell him that you are an American, not a mongrel."

It was nice to hear Ma say "American," because that is what we are: Americans. It is true proof of what this country is really all about; it is a melting pot that allows people from all races, religions, cultures, and walks of life to proudly call themselves Americans.

There were a few other mixed marriages in the neighborhood. The village was slowly becoming a melting pot of its own. I liked to think of the Shields kids as hybrids, a special mixture that was created by John and Annie Shields. It was kind of funny; even though we were half Scottish we really did not have much involvement with that part of our heritage. My father did not own a kilt, and he did not ask my mother to cook him haggis, finnan haddie, mutton, or roasted grouse. I will admit though that every once in a while my father would have a bowl of Campbell's Scotch Broth soup.

Our customs and traditions pretty much took the side of our Italian part of the family. My mother's family was where we get our way of life. I don't think that my father was not proud of his Scottish roots; it's just that he had been with my mother's side of the family for so long that he seemed to really enjoy being involved with the Italian traditions. But truth be told, every once in a while he made it a point to let us know that we kids had the Italian blood in us, not him.

The Christmas Pageant

We arrived at the Lincoln School, and as we got out of my father's car we realized that it had just begun to snow. With any kind of luck the snow might just keep up all night, and we would not have any school tomorrow. A snow day would be great!

We hurried to our classroom to report to our teacher, Mrs. DeMarco, so that she would know we were there. Some of the kids had to put costumes on.

The kids in the choir just had to sit and wait until it was our turn to perform. We were doing a combined presentation with the fourth grade class. Combining the fourth grade class with the fifth grade class kind of moved the whole Christmas pageant along, but the whole process seemed to take forever as far as I was concerned.

Jackie was outside warming the car up. Ellen, Gloria, Tony, and Ma were going in Jackie's car to the pageant. Ma gave everyone a holler, "It has started to snow. Make sure you wear your boots."

As they all went outside to the driveway they got their first glimpse of Jackie's new car.

Tony was all excited and blurted out, "I'm riding shotgun."

Jackie got out of the car and in a polite, brotherly voice told Tony that Ma would be sitting in the front seat.

Tony looked at Jackie, and he immediately understood what he was saying. He then pushed the seat back, because it was a two-door car, so that Ellen and Gloria could get in the car first. Jackie may not have been home all that often, but when he was home he did a very good job of showing his little brothers how to be respectful. Jackie waited for Ma to get in the front seat, and then he closed the door for her.

Ma turned to Jackie and stared at him for a moment. Ma then told Jackie, "You look very handsome tonight."

Jackie had gone all out for Ma tonight. He had his black double-breasted naval officer's uniform on with the brass buttons on the front. He had on his white silk aviator scarf with his naval officer's cap with the gold anchor along with his full-length black topcoat with brass buttons. Jackie looked like Admiral Halsey about to take command of the aircraft carrier Forrestal.

As Jackie pulled the car out of the driveway onto Spruce Street, Ellen asked, "Jackie, do you remember how to drive in the snow? After all you've been in Florida for a long time."

Jackie replied, "Oh, I remember just fine, Ellen. Don't be nervous; I'll take it slow going down the Oak

Street hill. If I can handle an F7U Cutlass at five hundred miles an hour, I think I can handle a Mercury at thirty miles an hour in the snow."

So off they went to watch little Billy perform, or I should say sing, in the Lincoln School Christmas pageant. The short ride up and down Oak Street was uneventful, even with the snow starting to fall. Jackie pulled up in front of the door to the school and let everyone out.

Jackie then headed to the parking area to park his car. Jackie got out of the car and stopped to make sure that everything was perfect with his uniform and the way he looked. Jackie knew the drill; it was his time to show off for Ma, to let his mother be the ever-so-proud mother of the handsome naval aviator. Jackie knew that the entrance that he and Ma made into the school auditorium would be important to her.

Ma was waiting patiently for Jackie at the entrance to the school. Jackie took Ma by the arm and opened the door to the school auditorium. The entrance they made looked as if the Queen of England was entering the hall. Ma knew that all of her friends and neighbors would have their eyes on her as she made the entrance with her attractive naval officer and aviator son. Jackie looked as proud to be with Ma as Ma was to be with him.

They walked slowly to where Dad had saved them seats. Ma had her arm tucked between Jackie's elbow and forearm, clutching him tightly and not wanting to let him go. Ma was enjoying the moment immensely. Ma looked radiant as she made her entrance and walked down the aisle. Ma had a look on her face and a slight smile that kind of looked like the cat that just swallowed the canary.

As Ma and Jackie moved toward their seats they heard our next door neighbors Lois and Archie Marino say, "Merry Christmas, Annie and Jackie."

Ma turned and gave them a quick wave as Jackie let go of her arm and walked over to give Lois a kiss and shake hands with Archie as he wished them a Merry Christmas.

Jackie turned from Lois and Archie to return to his seat, and who was standing right there in front of him with his hand out but good old Mr. Benson, the janitor?

Jackie gave Mr. Benson a firm handshake as he asked Mr. Benson, "How have you been?"

Mr. Benson, looking a little bit nervous, replied, "I'm doing just great, sir."

"Well, you and your family have a wonderful Christmas," Jackie added.

Mr. Benson was standing there beaming from ear to ear with a big smile on his face as he proudly replied to Jackie, "You too, sir; you too."

At this point Jackie took a look around the auditorium and realized that all eyes were on him. Jackie could hear many of the parents whispering and he saw many people waving to him as if he was a newly elected government official or some kind of prominent celebrity. Ma was sitting there with that look of pride on her face. She understood that tonight she was the pride of the village with all of her family by her side.

I don't know how Mrs. DeMarco kept her sanity with twenty-four screaming students running around the room all hyped up on the events of the evening. It really must have been trying for her. Mrs. DeMarco was really a nice lady and a good teacher. She had a tough life; her husband was killed in the Ardennes Mountain region of Belgium during The Battle of the Bulge near the end of World War Two.

Mrs. DeMarco had two children that she has raised alone on a teacher's salary. She was around forty years old. I guess she was not all that old, but for me anyone over fifteen was old. She had an attractive face and a very pleasant smile, but if you looked deep into her somber brown eyes you could see a trace of sadness.

Mrs. DeMarco had a green sweater and a red dress on. She looked like the spirit of Christmas. She may have looked vivacious as she greeted all of the parents with a smile as they drop their kids off, but deep down in her heart she had an ache that she did her best to camouflage with a bright-eyed smile. Even though World War Two had ended many years ago, the woman that married young and had been so in love still mourned the loss of her husband and deep down inside there was a pain that she knew would never leave her. Mrs. DeMarco was one of many women that had this cross to bear in life as the Second World War took its toll on many families.

I was bored and fidgety, so I asked Mrs. DeMarco if I could go to the boys' room. She said, "Billy, it's okay to go to the boys room, but don't get lost between our classroom and the boys' room please."

I guess Mrs. DeMarco really did know me. I was the wanderer who liked to explore and was ever-curious and afraid that he just might miss something in life if he did not stop to investigate.

As I walked down the hall toward the boys' room I ran into Ronnie Capobianco. He was a year older than I was and he was in the sixth grade, but we were kind of friends. He was a wiry kid that was always on the move. Although he was in the sixth grade, he looked like he was much younger. He talked with a slight lisp, which made it hard to understand him sometimes. He explained to me that he was on a mission. He was planning on sneaking into the kitchen that was next to the auditorium where they made the coffee and kept trays of cookies.

He told me, "I'm going to steal some cookies, the ones they give the parents when they have coffee and cookies after the pageant is over. The parents stand around drinking and eating while they were waiting for their kids to get changed and stuff."

I told Ronnie, "You might get caught and get into trouble."

Ronnie just laughed and said, "Hey, Billy, why don't you come with me?"

I had never been one to shy away from a challenge, so I told Ronnie, "Sure, I'll tag along with you."

Needless to say all of a sudden I was a bit nervous and concerned about this little caper, but I didn't want Ronnie to see that I was nervous. Off we went down the long hallway that was so colorfully decorated for the Christmas festivities toward the kitchen and a bounty of cookies.

We went through the double doors at the end of the hall and down a couple of stairs to the back entrance to the school auditorium. Sure enough, there before us in the small room adjacent to the side entrance to the stage was the big coffee pot and next to the coffee pot were three trays of cookies.

The trays had Italian cookies, biscotti, anisette toast, cavallucci cookies, and there was even some of those little cannolis.

The trays of cookies looked like money sitting on the floor of a bank, and all we had to do was get around the corner to that little room. The cookie trays were all covered with wax paper, so the challenge was to get in the room, uncover the cookies, fill our pockets full of cookies, and then cover the trays back up with the wax paper and scoot on out of the room. Not so hard to do.

All of a sudden I found myself excited and energized. I was about to pull off a major heist with a sixth grader. If we were successful with this escapade it would surely boost my ranking among the upperclassmen at the Lincoln School. Ronnie led the way, and I followed him down the stairs and around the corner. We were going in! As we made the turn and were about to go in, the side door opened and through the door walked Mr. Benson, the school janitor, with a broom in one hand and a waste basket in the other.

"Good evening, Mr. Benson," both Ronnie and I said in unison.

Our voices cracked and gained an octave or two as we greeted Mr. Benson, the stocky old janitor at Lincoln School since 1942. He stared at us over his thick, horn-rimmed glasses. His full head of grayish-silver hair matched his grayish-silver mustache. The hairs on his upper lip kind of curled into his mouth. I'm sure he saw the mischievous look in our eyes and heard the great trepidation in our voices. He spoke to us with his Swedish accent. "Goot evenin' to yeah boys," he said to us as we made a quick turn toward the stairs so that we could hightail it out of there. As we begin to change direction Mr. Benson added, "Had yer eyes on dem cookies, did ya lads?"

Ronnie and I stood frozen in our tracks and then took one more look at the room with all the cookies. Then we looked at each other, and with a sheepish smile we just stood there looking like two deer caught in the headlights of an oncoming tractor trailer.

Mr. Benson just smiled and put his broom to the floor, which gave us the opportunity to scurry on out of there leaving like two mice that just got their tails chopped off in a mouse trap!

Ronnie and I headed down the hall with what was left of our tails between our legs and our pride badly tarnished. We both agreed that Mr. Benson was a cool guy. He could have hung us out really good if he wanted to. My brother Jackie was right; Mr. Benson was a good guy.

I got back to the classroom and sure enough Mrs. DeMarco asked, "What took you so long, Billy? Was the door to the boys' room locked?"

I replied quickly, "No, Mrs. DeMarco, there was a big line in the boys' room, and I had to wait my turn"

I slowly sat back in my chair with my heart pounding and a look of guilt plastered all over my face.

In our segment of the Christmas pageant the combined fourth and fifth grade classes would be performing a brief synopsis of the birth of Jesus. Our class would have Mary and Joseph in the stable where Jesus was born, and there would be shepherds approaching the stable to see the baby Jesus. As the shepherds reached the stable the choir would sing a couple of Christmas carols.

We had been told by our music teacher and the director of the pageant, Mrs. Louden, "This portion of the pageant will be very dramatic with an operatic accompaniment."

Geez, could you get any cornier? It's just a bunch of kids looking and sounding like morons so that their parents would have something to talk about during the holidays.

I was beginning to settle down now after my harrowing experience with Ronnie Capobianco. I was sitting here watching the actors and actresses put their costumes on.

As I watched, I could not help but notice Jane Finch; she was a perky little girl, a little smaller than the other girls in our class. Jane was very pretty and a good pick to play Mary. She was a dead ringer for the Virgin Mary at ten years old. Like Mrs. DeMarco, Jane Finch had her share of sorrow in her young life. Jane's brother John drowned in a freak accident on the banks of the Aberjona River.

Jane's brother John was one of my brother Tony's best friends. John Finch, my brother Tony, and Paul Deprisco were coming home from an afternoon religion class at Saint Mary's school. On their way home they cut through the back of Saint Mary's school campus and stopped by the Aberjona River to throw rocks and play.

Tony had to leave as he had to deliver newspapers, but John and Paul stayed at the river bank and started floating rafts that they made out of twigs and sticks. The story I heard from Tony was that one of the rafts they made was floating down stream and got stuck on a lily pad. John Finch leaned over to dislodge the raft that was stuck and slipped and fell into the river. The rapid current took John out quickly, and because he had so many clothes on he got sucked under the water and drowned.

The death of John Finch was devastating to the community. John's family owned a corner grocery store and meat market on Washington Street and were very well respected and liked by everyone in the neighborhood. The death of John saddened the whole town. My brother Tony had a hard time getting over the death of a good friend at such a young age.

Although Jane Finch had suffered a great loss, she was still able to smile and go on. I admired her for being able to endure such a tragic event in her young life and still be able to smile.

John Foggerty was playing Joseph this year. He was Irish and a cousin of Jane Finch. John was tall and skinny with freckles and blondish brown hair. He was a real nice kid. Although there were many Italians in the village there was also a sprinkling of Irish that lived there. The fact that there were Irish in the neighborhood helped me to understand that not everyone in the village had macaroni on Wednesday nights. I have learned that some families eat red cabbage and potatoes, but that didn't really make them any different.

At long last, we got the call. From the front of the classroom Mrs. DeMarco announced, "It is time for us to perform. We are to march down the hall, single file to the back entrance of the stage."

Right next to the cookies, I thought.

"When we are announced by Mrs. Louden, we are to enter the auditorium single file and take our designated places on the bleachers next to the stage. The actors and actresses will already be on the stage behind the curtain."

I guess that all of the military stuff that took place during the Second World War had caused the grown-ups of the world to institute the single file rule in all of the elementary schools.

All of a sudden a feeling of panic started drifting through the classroom as Mrs. DeMarco explained the procedures. To most of the kids this whole pageant thing was kind of stupid, but it still meant that we had to be out there performing in front of our parents and siblings. In my family, all eyes would be on little Billy. I was sure my brother Tony would be in the audience making faces at me and trying to get me to laugh. I know that Aunty Sue would be watching my mouth to make sure that I get all words of the song sung correctly.

I wanted to look good and not screw up because the most important person would be out there watching, and that was my big brother Jackie. I wanted Jackie to be as proud of me as I was of him.

The fact that I had not been paying much attention to what had been going on was becoming clearly evident. I had spent way too much time letting my mind wander to what I might be getting for Christmas, rather than listening to Mrs. Louden during the many rehearsals that we had.

The first song that we were going to sing was "Lo How a Rose E'er Blooming." Geez, you would think that she would have picked a song like "Jingle bells" or "Deck the Halls" or something a little more traditional. How was I supposed to know the words to a song that I had sung like three times?

The second song we were going to sing was another winner: "While Shepherds Watch Their Flock by Night." Where the heck did she come up with these songs? I swear Mrs. Louden picked two songs that she knew we would never be able to remember the words to. Well at least I didn't know the words. I can't speak for all the other members of the choir. I just hoped that the lights in the auditorium were dim enough so that no one could see that I did not know the words to the songs.

We left the classroom and started to march single file down the dimly lit corridor. The way the kids were trudging down the hall and with everyone being so quiet you would think that we were all being led to one of those Nazi slaughterhouses that were so infamous during the Second World War. I swear if I turned the corner and saw a huge flag with a Nazi swastika, I was going to run like hell!

There we were walking past the room with the cookies on our way to the big show. Mr. Benson was standing right out in front of the cookie room with his broom in his hand. He looked like a guard watching Fort Knox. As we filed past Mr. Benson he gave me a wink. The time had come for us to perform.

I walked slowly behind Bonnie Pivera as we took our designated places on the risers. Bonnie was a very tall and buxom fifth grade girl. Standing next to Bonnie I looked like a dwarf. It's kind of funny how in the fifth grade some of the girls start to develop, and some of the girls look like awkward little feminine boys. It was good that Bonnie was standing next to me; she would attract more attention because she was so tall. What a great stroke of luck.

Ah, it looked like the choir gods were with me. I did not feel so concerned about not knowing the words to the songs. With the tall drink of water next to me I had nothing to fear. I was ready to enjoy the moment.

Oh no, oh no, what was happening to me! All of a sudden I had this sharp pain in the pit of my stomach. I could feel a slow rolling sensation in my gut. The gods were no longer with me. They had left me for who knows who? Maybe Bonnie Pivera, maybe Ronnie Capobianco? All I knew was that it appeared that my mother's meatballs or something had gotten me. I had this gurgling going on in my stomach. It sounded like a coffee pot percolating. I could feel this buildup of gas going on inside of me; oh no, I had to fart!

What a curse! What a most inopportune time to get hit with what my Grandfather so eloquently called "the bella gagatha pains." I was panicking; I was under tremendous pressure. I felt like I was about to explode!

Grandpa was renowned for his "bella gagathas." He had worked very hard at perfecting the process. With his wooden leg and a bit of a distance to travel to get to the bathroom before reaching relief, Grandpa had to prepare well in advance for his bowel movements. I unfortunately did not have that luxury at that moment. It was not like I could raise my hand and ask Mrs. Louden if I could be excused because I needed to take a dump. This was definitely not a good situation to be in. If I could just squeeze out a fart, it would help alleviate some of the pressure that had built up.

I had the solution, I would wait until we began to sing, then ever so slowly and cautiously I would attempt to let out one of those silent but deadly farts. With any kind of luck this would allow me some much-needed relief from the ungodly pains that I was experiencing.

We all began to sing. The first part of the song was very quiet. I had to wait. I had to endure until the tempo of the song livened up and the voices of the choir got louder. I had to wait just a few more seconds. The song was beginning to get louder; oh yes, oh yes, I felt it coming, oh my, I began letting it out, slowly, it is working, the gas was escaping, I only hoped that

I didn't crap myself! Oh yes, it was coming out nicely. The gas was escaping. I started feeling better right away. But wait; there was a foul odor. What was this God-awful smell coming up from between my legs? Oh God, it really did reek. What an awful smell! What was I to do?

Then it came to me; I'll turn my head very quickly and look at Bonnie Pivera. I would give her that evil look you know the kind you give someone when you catch them picking their nose in public. I would turn the attention toward Bonnie so that when everyone started getting a whiff of the God-awful fart they would turn around to see where it was coming from and they would see me giving Bonnie that evil look. This was genius. I was thinking that I just might get out of the predicament. If I pulled it off right, everyone will think that Bonnie Pivera cut the cheese and let the fart out.

This was great. It was actually working! Bobby Melo, who was in the second row, must have gotten a whiff of it because he turned around and looking back at Bonnie and then he looked at me.

Bobby saw me giving Bonnie "the look." He thought that she let it out. Everyone was turning their head around and looking back at us. I was looking at Bonnie and saw that her face was turning bright red; I didn't know how everyone kept singing. The smelly fart had been such a distraction. I even think that Mrs. Louden got a whiff of it because she had this pained look on her face as she waved her hands to the tempo of the music. Ah, but the show did go on!

Sledding

The Christmas pageant was a big event for the Shields family. My mother had a chance to relax for a little while and she also had the opportunity to show off her handsome young naval officer son, while her youngest performed so wonderfully in the choir. I guess whoever said the best things in life are free must have known the Shields family.

As we came outside from the pageant it was just about 9:30 p.m., and it was snowing like crazy. I turned to Steve and Bobby, and with a very big smile, I yelled, "Snow day tomorrow!" With the pageant behind us and only four days until Christmas, things were beginning to shape up for what looked like a very nice holiday season. The day after the pageant was Thursday, and on Friday there was only a half day of school, so if we got the day after the pageant off we would only have half a day of school left before the Christmas break. This was too good to be true!

Ma was going to ride home with Daddy, so I got to ride home with Jackie. Jackie had to brush the snow off the windows of the car before we got going.

When Jackie got in the car he told us, "I'm not used to brushing snow off of the car."

The snow was something he would have to get used to while he was home. The short ride from the Lincoln School to 79 Oak Street was going to be just a little more interesting than the ride Ellen, Gloria, and Tony experienced on the way to the pageant.

We made it out of the school parking lot okay, but as we start to drive up Oak Street hill the back wheels of Jackie's car began to spin right in front of the Bellini's house. Without missing a beat, Jackie down shifted the car to low gear, and the next thing we knew the back wheels caught and began to pull us up the hill.

Tony, who was not too far from acquiring his driver's license, asked, "Jackie, how did you get the wheels to stop spinning?"

Jackie explained to Tony, "This car has what's called posi-traction, which, when it is engaged, allows the axel to turn the wheels at a slower speed so it creates immediate traction. It's a new feature that just came out in the 1957 Mercury."

The rest of the ride home was as smooth as silk. We pulled into the driveway just behind my father. Dad backed his car into the shed so that he could pull straight out in the morning. We had a two-car garage, but for some strange reason, it was never used.

The garage was an old horse stable that was converted into a garage many years ago by the Barrone family, which owned the house before we did. My parents bought the house from the Barrone family right after World War Two. My father sent his pay home while he was away during the war, and my mother saved the money so that they could buy the house. My parents paid cash for the house and bought it just after my dad came home from the war.

The old horse stable/garage was kind of short for modern automobiles, so it was difficult to fit a full-sized car in the garage. It looked kind of funny that we had a garage but the cars were never parked in it. Dad built a shed attached to the garage and parked his car there. It was an open shed, but it protected the car from being snowed on. Jackie parked his car in front of the door on the left hand side of the garage.

We got out of the car and start walking toward the house. I was walking and kind of daydreaming without a care in the world, saying a Hail Mary under my breath as I was praying for it to keep snowing all night so that we could have the next day off from school.

Then, from out of nowhere and totally by surprise I got hit in the back of the head with a snowball! I was startled, to say the least, and stung by the speed of the snowball that hit me right in the back of the neck just under my cupolini. The snow immediately started to melt, and I could feel the freezing water running down the back of my neck.

I instantaneously turned around, and just as I was about to yell at Tony, figuring that Tony was the one that just threw the snowball, I saw Jackie with a big smile on his face and another snowball in his hand. Tony was smiling as well, but my instincts told me that it was Jackie that threw the snowball. I quickly reached down and picked up a handful of snow and made a snowball and chucked it has hard as I could at Jackie.

The next thing I knew I saw Ellen throwing a snowball at Tony. Gloria was making a snowball and throwing it at Ellen. Here we were in the backyard at almost ten p.m. and having a full-blown snowball fight!

Ma and Daddy were near the back door and laughing like crazy as they stood there and watched their kids as they threw snowballs at one another.

Ma yelled to us, "Be careful; I don't want to see anyone get hit in the eye."

After throwing snowballs at each other for a few minutes, Jackie took off his white silk scarf and began to wave it in the air, saying, "I surrender; I surrender!"

We were all covered with snow as the skies continued to dump snow on us and the wind began to blow harder. We all laughed and headed for the house.

I lay in bed drifting in and out of sleep, but I could hear this strange noise coming through my bedroom window. The longer I heard the noise the more familiar it became; I opened my eyes and I immediately bolted over to my window to look outside; oh my God, it was beautiful—snow, snow, and more snow!

The noise ... yes, I knew it sounded familiar ... it was the sound of a shovel scraping across the pavement of the driveway. Jackie, Tony, and Dad were outside shoveling.

It looked like a winter wonderland as I gazed out to the driveway. I saw about ten inches of snow, freshly fallen, puffy, fluffy snow. This had to be enough snow for them to call off school. But I would have to wait until they blew the no school horn at 7:15 a.m. for it to be official.

Having the day off from school would be awesome; it meant a full day of sledding on the Lincoln School hill. I got dressed quickly and first put on my thermal underwear because I figured I would probably be outside most of the day. I put on my dungarees, a plaid shirt, and over the shirt I put on one of Ma's knitted sweaters. I would be all set for a full day of sledding.

With the sound of the shovels scraping outside I figured I better get my tail out there and help, or I would never hear the end of it from Tony!

I hustled downstairs and saw Ma at the stove making coffee; I got hit with the wonderful smell of bacon frying in the pan. I said good morning to Ma. We were trained at an early stage in our lives that when we came downstairs in the morning we were to have smiles on our faces and with true sincerity say good morning to everyone that was in the kitchen.

This was a strict rule that my father had put in place, and he did enforce the rule. If you did not have a smile on your face and say good morning in a pleasant manner when you came downstairs in the morning he would tell you, "Okay, go back upstairs and come down again, and this time be in the right frame of mind."

I could not understand why he was so adamant about smiling and saying good morning, but no matter what his reasoning we did have to follow the rule.

I asked Ma, "Where is everyone?"

Ma let me know that Gloria was still in bed. Ellen had left for work already; she got a ride from Anna Deminico (who works with her at the telephone company and lived up the street), and Jackie and Tony were shoveling so that Daddy can get his car out and leave for work.

I put my coat and boots on and headed outside into the cold and snow. I must admit, shoveling snow was not one of my favorite things to do. However, Jackie was outside shoveling, and I wanted to spend as much time as I could with him while he was home. I've always been kind of ticked off that the boys had to shovel while Gloria lounged in bed. I wouldn't say she was lazy, but she is a girl, and girls seemed to get special dispensation when it came to working, especially shoveling snow. It seemed like there were special rules when it came to girls and work.

As I got outside I saw that most of the driveway was already shoveled; what luck! There was just the section at the end of the driveway where the plow dumped all the snow that needed to be shoveled. Upon my arrival in the driveway I was welcomed by my brother Tony, who greeted me with, "Hey chicken bones, did you decide to sleep until noon and wait for all the shoveling to be done before you came outside?"

"Ha ha, very funny, turd breath," I affectionately replied to him.

"That's okay, jerko, we saved the front walk for you to shovel," Tony let me know.

Just then I heard Jackie call over from the street where he was shoveling, "Hey, Billy! How are you doing this morning? Isn't this stuff great!"

"It sure is," I replied, as I turned to Tony and stuck my tongue out at him. Tony gave me the finger in reply.

Dad was cleaning the snow off of the front of his car that the wind blew under the front of the shed. The shed protected most of the car from the snow, but when it was really windy the snow would blow and drift under the front of the shed. Dad's car was warming up. I could see the exhaust coming from the back of the car. Dad pulled the car out from under the shed. He would leave it running to warm up while he had breakfast. Tony and Jackie were almost done shoveling where the plow came so I figured I better hurry up and shovel the front walk so that I could go in and have breakfast with everyone.

The snow was very light and fluffy, which was good. The cold temperature made the snow light, so it was really easy to shovel. Shoveling the front walk was a breeze. I'd be done in no time. It was really cold out. It might have warmed up a degree or two from the night before, but it was still very cold. I kind of wonder why I even have to shovel the front walk; it's not like anybody ever used it. Well, the mailman used the front walk when he delivered the mail, so I guess that's why I had to shovel it. It did seem like a lot of work for just one guy.

I finished shoveling in just a few minutes. I hurried up and walked from the front walk around the side of the house to the back door. It was kind of eerie being out in the snow all alone. You could hear the wind whistling through the barren trees, and the snow made a crunching noise as you walked on it. When I got in the back porch I unbuckled the snaps on my galoshes and took them off, then I took off my coat and hung it up so it would dry.

I walked in the kitchen from the back porch and immediately got hit with the aroma of fresh brewed coffee, the scent of bacon, and a faint hint of the smell of burnt toast. When all of those breakfast fragrances mix together they are heavenly. I saw everyone sitting at the table eating breakfast. Even Queen Gloria had decided to arise and honor us with her presence. I quickly sat down. Ma brought me a plate of scrambled eggs, toast, bacon, and a glass of orange juice.

Breakfast was big in our house. Well, I guess you could say every meal was big for us. Ma always seemed to have something good on the table for breakfast every morning when I came downstairs. I swear that Ma stayed up half the night making breakfast rather than sleeping because whenever I came downstairs for breakfast, no matter what time it was, Ma had food on the table.

It was just a little past six thirty in the morning; Dad had the radio on, and we were listening to Bill Marlow on radio station WCOP. "Hey, you guys better listen up; the school closings are coming on in just a minute," Dad let us know.

The reading of the school closing was always a traumatic event for Gloria, Tony, and me because we lived in Winchester, which is at the end of the alphabet, and they announced the school closings alphabetically. We always had to wait until the end of the list to find out if we had school or not. Even with all the snow that we had the superintendent of schools in Winchester just might throw us a curve ball and have us attend school.

There they go; they were starting: Abington, Arlington, Attleboro, Avon, Belmont, Billerica, Bolton, Boston, Brighton, Burlington... and on and on they go... Gloucester, Groton, Harvard, Holden... this is torture... Natick, Newton, Newbury, Newburyport... I was dying... if I didn't hear Winchester soon I was going to faint... Plymouth, Quincy, Randolph, Reading, Rehoboth... oh yes, they were closing in... Somerville, Stoneham, ... Stoneham this was a really good sign. Stoneham was the town next to Winchester, and if they did not have school, chances were good Winchester would not have school. I said a quick Hail Mary and then continued to listen. Taunton. Where the heck was Taunton? I had never heard of half of these towns.

I was starting to break into a slight sweat waiting for them to call Winchester. I had that uneasy feeling, the kind of feeling you get when you have done something wrong and you are in the confession booth, and the priest was about to slide the window open.

I swear Bill Marlow was making some of these names up just to tease me... Tyngsboro... Tyngsboro! Now he was definitely making them up. Upton... Upton... what the heck town was next? Downton?... Wakefield, Walpole... yes we were getting close, finally... Waltham, Wellesley... Oh God, why were you tormenting me? Wilmington, Winchendon... Winchester. Yes, yes! He said Winchester; I had never heard such a beautiful word.

It was true music to my ears, a far cry better than "Lo How a Rose E'er Blooming." Great, we had the day off!

Dad was leaving for work and gave Ma a big kiss good-bye as she was washing the dishes. Jackie was reading the newspaper, and Tony was sitting in front of the television set picking his nose. Television started broadcasting for the day at seven o'clock in the morning. Arthur Godfrey would be coming on the television soon. I liked watching Arthur Godfrey; he had a good show. I sat on the couch and watched the test pattern with Tony while we waited for broadcasting to start.

We purchased our television set about a year and a half ago. Aunty Sue and Aunty Laura had a television for a few years. Before we got our television set we would go to the aunts' house to watch television if there was something good on.

We had a family meeting to discuss whether we should buy a television. My father, a true Scotsman, decided that he was perfectly content with listening to the radio. He felt that television sets were way too expensive, and that we should wait a few years for the price to come down.

Everyone in the family complained, so Ma stepped in and said, "I'll help pay for the television with some of my Avon money." (In addition to working at the laundry Ma also sold Avon products on the side.)

Jackie had saved some money from his summer jobs, so he said, "I'll pitch in as well for the price of the television."

Ellen, who had just gotten her job at the telephone company, said, "I will contribute too."

Everyone had been paying board or contributing to the "house" since we started earning money. Gloria, Tony, and I had been giving Ma money each week from our jobs, but the money we provided did not go toward the purchase of the television.

There were not a lot of shows to watch on television, but it was really fun to watch. I loved watching The Lone Ranger on Saturday afternoon and Superman on Friday nights. Most of the time there is nothing on at all, and they just had the test pattern and this very high-pitched whistling sound. There were shows for adults like Omnibus, Liberace, or Kate Smith. I hated those shows. Ma still listened to her soap operas on the radio. Tony and I listened to Amos & Andy and The Green Hornet on the radio, but television was the thing of the future. Since we got the television set they had already added a channel. We now got channel four, which is NBC; channel five, which is ABC; and channel seven, which is CBS.

At seven a.m. on the nose The Arthur Godfrey Show came on the air. Tony and I were watching television, and at precisely 7:15 a.m. the town of Winchester warning signal horn blew three short blasts. There was a pause and then three more short blasts. It was now official: The superintendent of the Winchester school system had canceled classes for the day! The reason that the town blew a horn and gave a signal that school was canceled was because although we had a full-time fire department, we also had volunteer firefighters, and when there was a fire in town they would blow the warning horn to identify where the fire was.

Each section of town had its own specific code, so when there was a fire they would blow that code so the volunteer firefighters would know where to go. Our section of town, the village, was identified by five long blasts and two short blasts. They repeat the code three times so that it was properly indicated to the volunteers.

The town blew the warning signal (two short blasts) every day at 7:30 a.m. and at 7:30 p.m. They blew the signal each day as a test to make sure that the system was working. You could pretty much set your watch by this signal every day. Blowing the no school signal was for the benefit of the people of the town that might not have a radio or for some reason did not have access to any other form of notification.

The town also had an air raid signal that was a siren and was set off every Saturday at Noon. This air raid siren was to let the towns people know if we were having an air raid. They tested the siren at noon every Saturday just to make sure that it is working. The air raid siren was different from the town warning signal.

The air raid siren was very loud and sounded like a fire truck's siren, only louder. They let it sound for three minutes. Even though it was Saturday noon and you knew the siren was going to sound, it still scared the heck out of you. I swear every time I heard the siren I automatically looked up in the sky and I expected to see Jap Zero's or Nazi Messerschmitt ready to drop bombs on us. It was a good thing that they had this air raid signal, because you never know if we are going to be attacked. We had air raid drills once a month in school, and they ran advertisements on the television of what to do if there was a nuclear bomb dropped.

We did have an incident that occurred in October on a Thursday afternoon that darn near scared me to death. I had come home for lunch, well, I went to Grandpa's house for lunch because we got out of school for lunch at 11:45 and had to be back at school by 1:00 p.m.

I had some leftover soup that Aunty Sue left for me and Grandpa in the refrigerator. I just had to heat it up on the stove. After I had my soup with Grandpa I headed back to school. I left Grandpa's house at 12:40, which gave me plenty of time to walk back to school.

As I was walking back to school I remember I was on Oak Street just before the intersection of Holland Street when the air raid siren went off.

Now please remember that it was Thursday at 12:45 p.m., not Saturday noon when the air raid siren usually went off. I have to admit, panic set in immediately! I was in a sticky situation, and I was not sure what to do.

The very first thing I did was look up at the sky. I thought for sure there would be a squadron of Russian MIGs flying overhead. I did not see any planes, but I kept thinking, Why would the air raid siren go off on Thursday at 12:45 p.m.?

The air raid siren eventually stopped. I still was not sure what to do. Should I go back to Grandpa's house? Should I go on to school? After much anguish, I decided on going to school.

When I got to school I found out that the air raid siren was a false alarm. The teachers let us know that there was no actual air raid. Well, I have to tell you, the false alarm of the air raid siren was a very harrowing experience!

If some demented government official from the town of Winchester was trying to put a scare into a little kid, he did an excellent job!

I continued to watch television with Tony for a few minutes, but after watching Halee Loki sing a Hawaiian song and Carmel Quinn sing an Irish song and watching Arthur Godfrey drink some Lipton tea, I figured I'd had enough television and it was time to hit the hills. After all, it was a "snow day," a rare day to be enjoyed doing nothing but sledding with the friends.

I went to the kitchen to call my friends and see if they were ready to go sledding. Ma was getting ready to go to work and putting on her coat.

I asked Ma, "Where's Jackie?"

Ma told me, "He is outside warming up his car. He is going to give me a ride to work this morning."

Ma was very happy that she was getting a ride to work and she did not have to walk down Shore Road after a snow storm. Shore Road is cold and desolate enough, but with the wind whipping the snow off of Judkin's Pond and into your face, it's more like a trek on the frozen tundra than a walk to work. I only hoped that it would be better in the afternoon when I had to deliver my newspapers.

As I picked up the phone to call Steve I realized what a different experience using the telephone was, as we no longer had to wait for an operator to say, "Number please." We recently switched over from using an operator to get a connection to having a dial on the phone.

The phone system had been completely revamped. Our phone number had been Winchester 6 -0431. The system had been changed so that our exchange was Parkview 9- 3243.

I don't know where they came up with Parkview for the exchange for Winchester. The towns next to us had changed as well. Medford was Export 5 and Woburn was Wells 3. I bet that someone at the phone company must have had some fun making up all of those new exchanges.

It sure was a lot faster using a dial rather than waiting for an operator. It seemed that whenever I used the phone the operator had an attitude. I think that they were trained to give little kids a hard time when ever a kid used the phone.

I could remember using the phone to call one of my friends, and I would get from the operator, "Young man, did your mother give you permission to use the phone?"

Being the polite young boy that I am I would always answer; "Yes, ma'am. My mother certainly did give me permission to use the phone."

I would like to have said, "Hey, lady, who gave you permission to be so crabby?" but I wasn't that kind of kid. Well I might have been that kind of kid, but I know for sure I'd get my hide tanned if I ever did say that to an adult!

The biggest change with the phone company was that instead of having a big black phone with a cradle that sits on a table, we had a pretty green phone with a dial that was attached to the wall. What progress!

I dialed Steve's phone number to see if he was going sledding. Steve's mother answered the phone, "Good morning, Billy. Are you happy to have the day off from school today?"

"I sure am," I replied.

"Hold on a second, and I'll get Steve for you," she said with a laugh.

Steve got on the phone.

"Hey, Steve, I told you we would have a snow day."

"You were right, Billy," he let me know.

"Isn't this great? We have the day off, and we can go sledding," I continue. "Let's go to the school yard and hit the hill."

"Sure, sounds like a great idea. Do you want me to get Bobby and come by your house?" he asked.

"Yeah, get Bobby and come on by," I answered firmly.

"Okay. Bobby and I will be by your house in a few minutes," he told me.

"I'll be ready." I slammed the phone down and got ready for sledding.

The Lincoln School yard had a great sledding hill. As you walked in the school yard just past the Guidos' house, on the right was the hill. It's not that steep, but it goes a long way. If you had a good sled, you could get around two hundred feet from top to bottom before you came to a stop. If you had a good sled and the runners were waxed you might get a little bit more. Some of the kids do not have a sled, so they used a cut-up cardboard box and slide on the cardboard. Some kids had those new round metal flying saucer things, but they were not as good as a sled.

My sled was old; it was a hand-me-down just like everything else I got. In a family with five children, it was standard procedure to pass things down to the youngest, I guess. I seldom got anything new. My sled was okay, but one of the slats was broken, so I fixed it with some electrical tape that I got from my dad's workbench. I think Grandpa brought the sled over with him from Italy; it was so old. All of the writing on the sled was worn off, so I had no idea what kind of sled it was. Old or not it still got me down the hill. I sat patiently waiting for Steve and Bobby to show up.

Steve and Bobby finally showed up. I guess Bobby had to take the clinkers out of the furnace before he could go sledding. This delayed their arrival. The clinkers were the little pieces of coal that do not burn in the furnace. You had to remove the clinkers with the ashes so that the furnace worked efficiently. Most families in the neighborhood had switched over to gas or oil for their heating, but Bobby's family still used coal in their furnace.

Bobby's family did not do that well; his father worked as a delivery man for Marino's bakery. He did not make a lot of money, and he really did not like his job. His father liked to take a drink more often than he should, which made him kind of mean at times. Life has not been easy for Bobby's family. His older sister came down with polio a year or so ago and almost died. Ever since his sister got sick his mother was always fussing over him and his sister because she was so worried about them getting sick.

Now that we were all ready to go, we headed out for the Lincoln School hill for some serious sledding. The walk seemed to take forever. I'm not sure if it was the anticipation of going sledding or all the clothes that I had on that was making the walk so slow. We made it up to the top of Oak Street, which was the hard part of the hike. We slogged our way down Oak Street, which was not nearly as slow as the walk up the hill. We entered the driveway to the school, and as we got past the Guidos' house, we got our first glimpse of the hill. Sure enough the hill was packed with kids sledding. It looked like half the school was there sledding.

As we began our climb up the hill I heard "Hey, Shields!" from the top of the hill. I looked up the hill and who did I see but Charlie Vassali, the paperboy that ranked on me at the news store and the toughest kid in the neighborhood. I looked at Charlie from the bottom of the hill. With all his winter clothes on he kind of looked like the guy we read about in history class, Jim Bridger, who was a great big, mean old mountain man that helped Lewis and Clark find their way west.

"Hey, Shields, come over here," Charlie yelled again.

I immediately became a little concerned as to why Charlie Vassali would be calling me over. I told Bobby and Steve, "I'll be right back, but keep an eye out for me in case something happens."

They both gave me this look of terror, and they said in unison, "You're on your own with Charlie Vassali."

I timidly walked over to where Charlie was standing. Charlie had this sheepish look on his face as I approached him.

The next thing I heard from Charlie was, "Hey, Shields, have some Christmas candy."

I was a little perplexed. I awkwardly replied with a very inquisitive response, "Huh?"

With a very matter of fact response Charlie let me know, "Sister Gertrudious had all these boxes of candy on her desk that kids gave her for Christmas, so when she wasn't looking I stole some."

I said, again with an even more inquisitive response, "You stole candy from a nun?"

"Yeah, I stole candy from a nun. What's the big deal?" Charlie responded.

"Geez, Charlie, if I eat this stolen candy from the nun would I go to hell or something? Do I have to tell the priest when I go to confession?" I asked.

"No, you idiot. Do you want some candy or not?" Charlie, even more annoyed, asked me.

Needless to say I took some candy. I knew that I could not refuse taking a piece of candy from Charlie Vassali, even if I would spend half an eternity in purgatory! "Thanks a lot," I said to Charlie as I put the candy in my mouth, I silently whispered to myself, Please, God, don't let me choke on this candy. Then I walked back over to Steve and Bobby.

When I finally got back over to Steve and Bobby, they were just coming back up the hill after they had already made their first run.

They both asked me, "What did Charlie want?"

"He stole some candy from the Nuns desk and offered me a piece," I told them. I was feeling so guilty that I spit out the candy I was eating and looked back to make sure that Charlie did not see me spitting it out.

I asked them, "How's the snow for sledding today?"

Bobby was using a wooden dough box that his father brought home from Marino's bakery.

It looked kind of dumb, but Bobby said, "Hey, the dough box works really well."

Steve was like me; he had a hand-me-down sled that his older brother Rocco gave him. Steve was the youngest in a family with four kids that barely made ends meet. He had his share of problems in his family as well. His mother did not work, and she was always complaining about the family not having any money and stuff. We never went over to his house to play because his mother was so crabby.

I got my sled and slid the runners back and forth in the snow to get the rust off of them. As I was about to push off and head down the hill I heard another voice call me, "Hey, Billy." It was John Foggerty.

I stopped and say, "Hey, John. How are you doing today?"

John was with his cousin Skinny Finch. Skinny goes to the Washington School, but he was spending the day at John Foggerty's house, so he was obliged to go sledding on the Lincoln School hill. We had an ongoing rivalry with the Washington School kids. Each year, during the last week of school, we had the Lincoln/Washington jamboree. This jamboree was a series of events like three legged races and sack races and stuff like that where we competed against the Washington School kids for prizes and trophies.

This was a big event every spring, so both schools tried their hardest to win. We aren't best of friends with the Washington School kids, but Skinny was okay, and he's John's cousin, so we Lincoln School kids cut Skinny some slack.

Finally I lay down on top of my old sled and got ready to head down the hill. What an experience to be zooming down the hill with your face about six inches off of the snow. It was a great feeling to have the wind whiz by your face as you whooshed down the hill. My old sled made it about three quarters of the way down the slope. Not a bad first run for an old clunker of a sled.

I enjoyed my ride down the hill so much that as I was heading back up the hill, I didn't pay much attention to the commotion that was going on near the driveway that heads into the school yard. I saw that all of the kids had stopped sledding, and they were gathered around a car that was parked just past the Guidos' house.

As I looked closer I realized that the car the kids were congregating around was a Blue 1957 Mercury Monterey. Hey, wait a minute; that's my brother Jackie's car! What the heck is he doing here?

I dropped my sled and started running over to where all the furor was taking place. Sure enough, standing there in his official brown leather bomber jacket was my brother Jackie. He looked really handsome, standing there with his leather bomber jacket that had a patch with the United States Navy insignia on one side of his chest and a patch over his heart that read

"Lieutenant John A. Shields." He really looked like a movie star standing there.

As I approached the scene I saw that Jackie was talking to all of the kids. They were asking him all sorts of questions about what it was like to fly jet airplanes and what it was like flying in air shows doing stunts and flying in formation. Jackie patiently answered each and every question that he got asked. Standing in the front of the group was Charlie Vassali with a big grin on his face. Charlie was standing next to Jackie looking like he was his official press secretary. Charlie scanned the crowd, nodding to those that wanted to ask a question.

I got to the car and asked Jackie, "What are you doing here?"

When Jackie saw me he smiled and headed to the back of his car and opened the trunk. Jackie reached inside of the trunk and pulled out a brand new, shiny red with polished wood Flexible Flyer sled. I could not believe it; a genuine, honest to goodness Flexible Flyer, the Cadillac of all sleds, the best that money could buy, a real Flexible Flyer! I was shocked when he put the sled in my hands. I was so surprised that you could have knocked me over with a feather!

Jackie looked at me with a smile and said, "I thought you could use this today."

"I sure could," I replied with a giant smile on my face.

"Well, here, have some fun, but don't get hurt," he added.

I was totally lost for words. I thanked Jackie and gave him a big hug. He hugged me back and gave me an extra squeeze. Jackie looked at me and said, "This was an early Christmas present."

I was standing there with a huge smile on my face. I took a look at all the kids that were over next to Jackie's car, and I could see this astonished look on all of their faces. Skinny Finch actually had a strand of drool dripping from his mouth. It was open wide in amazement. Steve and Bobby were staring at me with this look of why can't I have a big brother like that? Charlie Vassali was standing there in his Jim Bridger mountain man outfit with a look of bewilderment on his face.

I again thanked Jackie and let him know how much I would enjoy sledding with the beautiful sled.

Then Jackie said to me, "Hey, Billy, I'll help you do the paper route again tonight; be home around three o'clock, and I'll drive you down to the news store. I want to say hello to Mr. Mullen anyway."

"That's great; I'll be home at three," I let him know.

Jackie gave me another hug, and then got in the car and waved good-bye to me and all the kids. We all waved good-bye to him as he pulled out of the school yard.

Wow; what an unbelievable day! My new Flexible Flyer rode like a rocket ship down the hill, or should I say like an F7U Cutlass! I flew down the Lincoln School hill as if I was floating on top of the snow. The darn thing went so fast that it took forever to walk back up the hill. I was king of the mountain that afternoon. Charlie Vassali might have been the biggest on the mountain, but I was the king.

I did come to my senses though and let some of the other kids take a ride on my new sled. I let Charlie use the sled first; after all it's always a good thing to have Charlie on your side as you never know when he might be helpful to a kid of ten years old. I let Bobby and Steve have a few runs down the hill as well. Seeing I had the new flexible flyer I let Bobby use my old sled for the rest of the day so he didn't have to use the bread dough box. All the kids loved my sled and thanked me for letting them use it.

The walk back home made me feel like a true celebrity. All of the kids thought Jackie was so cool for giving me the new Flexible Flyer. The kids told me that they wished they had a brother like Jackie. Deep down inside I was very thankful that I did have a brother like Jackie, and believe me, I did not want to share him with anyone!

A Night Out with the Boys

I got home from sledding with a permanent smile, as if it was tattooed on my face. I took off my wet clothes and changed into another pair of dungarees to get ready to do my paper route. I had a quick cup of hot chocolate and a couple of cookies. No sooner did I finish my snack than Jackie walked through the door. "Hey, Billy, how did that sled work out for you?"

"It was fabulous!" I exclaimed. "I had the most fun ever. I didn't want to leave the hill."

"Well, I'm sure that there will be more snowstorms and many more days to sled down Lincoln School hill before winter is over," he replied. "Are you ready to do the paper route? You've got to keep the customers happy; this is tip week, remember."

I let him know, "I sure am ready; I've been waiting a long time for this week to come."

We headed out to Jackie's car to proceed downtown to pick up the papers. The backseat of Jackie's car was filled with beautifully wrapped Christmas presents.

Jackie always did things right; all the presents were wrapped with bright red and green foiled wrapping, the expensive kind that makes them seem so much better than the ones wrapped with plain old paper wrapping.

Jackie let me know, "I went to Medford square to pick up a few presents for the family. The two biggest stores in Medford, Gorin's and Gilchrist's, were packed with shoppers. I forgot what being in a city around Christmas time was like. Pensacola is a lot different than Boston, and there are not as many people. I have quite a few presents here, so after we do the paper route you can help him bring the presents in the house and put them under the Christmas tree."

It was almost 3:30 p.m. by the time we pulled up in front of the news store. I told Jackie, "I'm going to grab the two-wheel dolly and head up to meet the 3:45 train to pick up the late edition of The Record American."

He told me, "I'm going to go into the store and say hello to Mr. Mullen while you pick up the papers."

Today was not as cold as yesterday when I was waiting for the train, or perhaps I just had a warm feeling knowing that I was going to be driven around my route again by Jackie. The flashing sign at the National Bank Building showed twenty-eight degrees, but I had the warm feeling of a summer day inside of me.

Most of the paperboys, including me, felt that Mr. Mullen was a really crabby old guy. Actually Charlie Vassali called him an old bastard, but I knew better than to refer to him that way, well not to his face anyway. He was a chubby little man with a red face and no hair. He always seemed to be mad, and he never smiled at anything.

Mr. Mullen owned the news store and had the franchise for distributing the newspapers in Winchester. His two sons also worked at the News Store. They weren't as bad as the father, but they were no box of chocolates to deal with. It always seemed like an ongoing battle existed between the paperboys and the Mullen family. There was one other guy that worked at the news store, Eddie Quinn. He was a really nice guy. He never gave us kids a hard time, and he didn't try to cheat us like the Mullens did. Actually I guess I should be happy that I have the paper route and that I'm making a few bucks.

Mr. Mullen seemed to be nicer to grown-ups than he was to kids. I guess once you get older and don't have a paper route anymore, like Jackie, Mr. Mullen becomes nice to you. I guess I will understand things better when I get older. Maybe I just had to learn to accept people for who they were, even if they were a little crabby.

I got back from the train station just as Jackie was saying good-bye to Mr. Mullen. Jackie shook hands and smiled as he waved good-bye to the man Charlie Vassali called "the old bastard." I think I could get used to calling him that myself.

I got my newspapers and hustled out to Jackie's car. I moved the presents over that were in the backseat. Then I put the papers beside the gifts and jumped in the front seat. I paused for a moment and took in that new car scent of Jackie's Mercury Monterey. I vaguely remember the new car smell when Dad got the Studebaker. That was a long time ago. I made a silent vow to myself that someday I was going to get a new car and enjoy that new car aroma myself.

It was December 22 and just a day away from when I did my weekly collections for the newspaper. Tomorrow would be the big payday. The abbondanza of the year; the day I had waited for since I took the paper route over from my brother Tony.

I had suffered through more pain than you could imagine while performing my nightly paper route. Because collection day was always on a Friday and most of my customers were Catholic and could not eat meat on Friday, I had to endure the smell of just about every one of my customers frying fish of some sort when I knocked on the door, and they brought me into their kitchen.

The smell of frying fish permeated my clothes and seemed to stick to my skin. I would come home on Friday nights and my mother would give me the ole caputza (you stink). I was beginning to get a complex when I got home on Friday nights!

With sixty customers that would most likely tip me at least a buck apiece at Christmas and then there were a couple of big tippers that would tip me more than a buck, that might be able to bring me close to seventy-five bucks!

I would have to turn over at least half of my money to Ma for the house, so I could come out with … hmmm, wait a minute while my internal abacus does the calculations … close to forty bucks, all to myself. What a payday; what a score; this haul might come close to the Brinks caper! Well not quite that much, but a tidy sum of money nonetheless.

I did my Christmas shopping at F. W. Woolworth's, the old five and dime. I planned on getting everyone the best gift in the world. As I said, this was going to be a great Christmas!

Just as we were finishing the paper route, Jackie told me, "I'm going out with my buddies tonight, so I have to hustle home and get ready. I'm only home for a few days and want to see the buddies that I grew up with."

I asked him, "What are you going to be doing, and where are you going?"

Kids my age do ask a lot of questions. Unfortunately when kids like me asked a lot of questions, most adults just sloughed them off and paid them lip service. They gave you some foolish response like, "Oh, you don't need to know" or "When you get bigger you'll understand." I was used to those kind of responses because I was a kid.

I actually didn't expect much of a response from Jackie, but he was kind enough to let me know: "I'm going out with Mario Mastrano, Sonny Luongo, Bill Maggiori, and Jimmy Valenti. We are going to start the evening out at the Sons of Italy Club on Swanton Street." He goes on, "We are going to catch up on old times and share stories of about the escapades that have taken place since the last time we were together."

Jackie had not seen his buddies since the last time he was home, so they had a lot to catch up on. He told me, "After catching up over a couple of beers at the

Sons of Italy, we'll probably go out somewhere to get a cup of coffee and something to eat"

I felt kind of important that my older brother had taken the time to tell me what he and his friends were going to do. I was not used to anyone actually paying attention to me!

Ma made another one of her great suppers. It was Thursday night, so we were having lamb chops, peas, mashed potatoes with gravy, one of Ma's great salads, and of course that fresh Marino's scalli bread. I had gotten much better with peas. I had always hated eating peas. To me peas tasted like eating a piece of mushed up green construction paper. You know, the kind of thick paper you use to do projects on in school. Peas were just one step ahead of the most dreaded vegetable of all, lima beans. Yuk.

For the longest time, I would sit down to eat, then stuff all of the peas in my mouth and abruptly mumble, "I've got to go to the bathroom." But it really sounded like, "I blah blah to the blath broom." Then I would run to the bathroom, close the door, and quietly spit the peas (or lima beans, I did it with them as well) into the toilet. I don't think I was really tricking anyone, but they let me get away with it anyway.

On Thursday nights we most times had either lamb chops or pork chops, whichever Freddy Razaboni, the butcher, thought were better. Freddy seemed to dictate our meals sometimes because of what meat he had that looked better. I never quite got that term "looked better"; did that mean which lamb chop or pork chop smiled the best or had the best complexion? Oh well, something else I'll figure out when I get older. I could understand "tasted better," but looked better was just a little confusing.

Jackie told Ma that he was going out with the boys and that he would skip dessert because he and the boys were probably going to go out for coffee and something later on.

For dessert, Ma made a Bundt cake, one of those coffee cake things with crumbs on the top. It was pretty good, but not my favorite. Actually Gloria made the Bundt cake. She used one of those Duncan Hines premixed boxes where you just added water and an egg. Nothing like when Ma made a cake. Ma always started from scratch and added all sorts of good things like butter and cream and stuff like that. But then again, Gloria was helping out, so I should not have complained. At least I was getting something for dessert.

Jackie's buddies showed up at the house just after seven o'clock. They came into the kitchen and gave my mother a big hug, and they shook hands with my dad. They all give me a rub on top of my head and asked me how I was doing and mentioned how big I had gotten since they saw me last. Gloria and Ellen had gone out Christmas shopping, and Tony was upstairs supposedly doing his homework.

The guys sat down in the living room while they waited for Jackie to come downstairs. He had gone upstairs to change because he did not want to wear the black, navy-issued shoes he had on earlier. He liked wearing his black leather boots. They did look kind of cool. They weren't cowboy boots or anything like that;

he called them his dress boots. They were like eight inches high and let your pants leg go over them, so they really did not look like you had boots on at all. They were really shiny. But then again, Jackie said that in the Navy you always had to make sure your shoes were always shiny and clean.

Just before we sat down for supper tonight Ma took out her trusty old Kodak camera and decided to take some pictures of the family while we were all together. Ma's camera had a place where you put in the flash bulb. The place for the flash bulb kind of looked like a big silver funnel on the top of the camera. The flash bulbs that Ma used in the camera were about the size of an egg. When you took pictures in the house you had to use a flash bulb so it would be bright enough for the film to develop.

When the flash bulb went off you had to take it out of the funnel-shaped device and replace it with a new bulb. When a flash bulb went off and after it was used, it kind of looked like a big ugly grayish bubble.

Ma decided that she wanted to get a couple of snapshots of the boys before they went out, so she had her camera ready for when Jackie came downstairs.

Well, unbeknownst to anyone, before Jackie went upstairs to change his shoes, he took one of Ma's used flash bulbs with him. Ma, Dad, Jackie's friends, and I were sitting in the living room waiting for Jackie to come down the stairs.

We could hear Jackie as he started to come down the stairs; Jackie kind of had his head turned away from us as he got to the bottom of the stairs. All of a sudden Jackie turned toward the living room; he got to the bottom of the stairs, and sure enough the prankster had one of Ma's used flash bulbs stuck in his right nostril so it looked just like he had a giant snot hanging from his nose. Ma took a picture as we all laughed like crazy.

After the laughter died down Jackie, with a big smile on his face, took the flash bulb out of his nose and gave a big, "Hey, how are you guys doing? It's great to see you."

Jackie shook hands with Sonny Luongo first, then Bill Maggiori, then Jimmy Valenti, and finally Mario Mastrano. Jackie's friends seemed really happy to see him. They all had big grins on their faces. Both Ma and Daddy had big smiles on their faces as well. Ma asked the guys if they wanted a cup of coffee or anything; they all declined as they said they had just had dinner, but they all said thank you for offering.

It was nice to see Jackie together with the friends that he grew up with. Jackie went off to college right after he graduated high school and then went right into the navy, so he now only saw his buddies when he was home on vacation. I guess they do have a lot to catch up on.

Jackie was born right after my parents got married. I've heard the story that he was born nine months and two weeks after my parents' wedding day. Both Jackie and Ellen were born while my parents were living in Brighton, Massachusetts, which is a Boston neighborhood near Saint Elizabeth's Hospital and Boston College.

When Jackie was finishing the second grade and Ellen was completing kindergarten my parents moved to Winchester to live upstairs from Grandpa and Grammy in their second floor apartment. This was the move to the Italian section of Winchester (The Italian Village). It was the summer just before World War Two started.

When Jackie enrolled in the Lincoln School, he entered the third grade. Now you have to understand that the Lincoln School was made up of mostly the Italian kids in the neighborhood. Back when Jackie was there, some of them were first generation and could not speak English very well. Many of them had a hard time understanding what was going on in the classroom. After the first couple of weeks of being in the Lincoln School, Jackie was called to the principal's office.

As was always the case, there was a certain amount of trauma and anxiety associated with a visit to the principal's office. Jackie went in and sat down and waited to be called into her office.

"John," (that is his real name) Mrs. Wardsworth addressed him as she sat there very prim and proper, "we have been reviewing your test scores and class work, and we have determined that you are not being properly challenged in the third grade. Therefore, we are going to move you up to the fourth grade class."

Geez, what a lucky guy! Anyway, Jackie skipped the third grade. Then, when Jackie graduated the sixth grade from Lincoln school and went down to the junior high school, it happened again!

Jackie was moved from the seventh grade to the eighth grade. Again, they indicated that he was not being challenged. Now some of those kids I mentioned that are first-generation Italians at the Lincoln school had to repeat a few grades. This put Jackie at somewhat of a disadvantage because he was always younger than most of the kids in his grade. I remember my sister Ellen mentioning that some of those kids in the Lincoln School were actually shaving when they were in the sixth grade.

Jackie was a little younger than some of his friends, but most of them were close in age. For instance, Sonny Luongo was a year behind Jackie in high school but a year older than Jackie. The same was true for Mario Mastrano. Jimmy Valenti was two grades behind Jackie in school but the same age, and Bill Maggiori was a year younger than Jackie. They all grew up in the same neighborhood and were very close as friends growing up.

All of them have one thing in common that will stay with them the rest of their lives. I think this one single event that took place in their childhood is the glue that will never separate them.

The event I am talking about happened on the evening of August 14, 1945, better known as VJ Day—victory in Japan. The announcement on the radio, just after six o'clock in the evening, signaled the end of World War Two.

Apparently when the announcement was made that the war was over the village went wild. There were horns honking and lights blinking and all sorts of mayhem in the neighborhood. Jackie was twelve years old. He and his friends immediately joined the celebration.

There were Jackie, Sonny, Mario, Bill, Jimmy, and Tommy Cantella, who participated in the big celebration.

The boys went down to the end of Spruce Street next to Shore Road where there was a swamp. All of them picked a bunch of cats o' nine tails. These are reeds that grow up from the swamp. They are about five feet tall. At the top of the reed it has a section about six to eight inches long of a soft brown fuzzy, furry type material. Kind of like a hot dog bun on the end of a stick.

Well the boys took the cats o' nine tails and started up the street. When they got as far as Mrs. Napoli's house at the end of shore road, they ran into Mrs. Napoli's daughter Maria, who went to school with the boys. Maria was holding a sparkler that was spraying sparks everywhere and looked very festive.

Tommy Cantella had what he thought was a very bright idea. He told Maria Napoli, "Go into your father's barn and get us guys some kerosene."

Maria, being a mischievous young girl, and having a little thing for Tommy, who was a handsome kid, did not hesitate to run into her father's barn and bring out a can of kerosene. Tommy Cantella's idea was to dip the end of the cats o' nine tails into the kerosene and then light them on fire so that they will look like a giant torch or a sparkler.

Perhaps it was the excitement of the wonderful news and the overall mayhem that was taking place, but the other boys threw caution to the wind and went along with Tommy's idea.

The boys all dipped their cat o' nine tails in the kerosene. Maria Napoli promptly lit Tommy Cantella's cat o' nine tails on fire with another sparkler that she had lit. I guess it happened really quickly. Before Maria could light any more cats o' nine tails, as Tommy held the makeshift torch up in the air the top of Tommy's cat o' nine tails fell off. Because it was soaked with kerosene, which burns like crazy, it fell onto his head and shirt, immediately catching Tommy on fire. The other boys quickly dropped their cats o' nine tails to help Tommy, but by this time the fire had totally consumed Tommy's clothes.

Tommy started screaming and freaking out. He ran as fast as he could toward the swamp, but the faster Tommy ran the more intense the fire became. Tommy fell down just short of the swamp and rolled around on the ground for a few seconds and then he did not move. Jackie and his friends ran over to try and do something to help Tommy, but it was too late. It happened in the blink of an eye. Celebration turned into tragedy in just a fleeting moment. Tommy Cantella was dead.

I've heard the story a few times, but I've never asked Jackie about it. I guess the trauma never leaves you when you see one of your best friends die right in front of you.

So the boys, Jackie, Sonny, Mario, Bill, and Jimmy, will always have that horror to live with, something that they can never forget. So they get together when they can and reminisce about the good times and console one another over the bad.

Both my brother Jackie and my brother Tony lost close friends when they were young. Jackie lost Tommy Cantella and Tony lost John Finch. I sure hope this doesn't put the maleficio (Italian for evil spell) on any of my friends!

Jackie and his friends, Sonny, Bill, Jimmy, and Mario, left our house and got into Jackie's car. They were quite impressed with his new wheels.

Jackie later shared with me what they did on their night out: Jackie decided to take a tour of Winchester, to drive past the places they had such fond memories of when they were younger. They first drove past the swamp at the end of Spruce Street and silently remembered Tommy Cantella.

Then they drove by the high school on the corner of Mystic Valley Parkway and Washington Street, then through the center of town, up past the spa on the corner of Main and Water Street, and then down Cross Street past Leonard's Beach.

These are all places that the boys had memories of when they were together growing up in the village. They even drove through the West Side of town to see how the other half was living, and then they drove past the Winchester Country Club, where all the old Yankees are members.

Sonny had worked one summer as a caddie at the Winchester Country Club. He would tell stories of how some of the old Yankees with all that money were so cheap when it came to giving a tip to the caddie at the end of a round of golf.

The boys got to the Sons of Italy Club at the top of Swanton Street at just about eight o'clock. Sonny and Mario were members, so it was okay for them to bring their friends into the club. All of the old timers that were at the club knew the guys and made it a point to come over and shake hands with Jackie and to ask him how things were going with flying jets in the navy. Jackie, always the respectful gentleman, made it a point to be sincere and to spend a few moments sharing his experience with flying jets and the navy in general with each man that shook his hand.

Most of the guys from the neighborhood belonged to the Sons of Italy and are veterans of some branch of the service. Many of them served in the Second World War. They were very respectful to anyone that served our country. As a matter of fact, Sonny Luongo had joined the Marine Corps as soon as he graduated high school in 1951. Sonny was in the First Marine Division, and in 1952 he fought in the Battle of Bunker Hill (Hill 122) in western Korea. This was the first major ground action fought in western Korea. Sonny did not like to talk much about his stint in the Marine Corps. He was very humble and felt that his time in the service was just something that he was supposed to do.

Sonny was a handsome guy. He stands about five foot nine inches tall and had an olive complexion and a full head of wavy black hair. Sonny had an infectious smile that made you stare at him the minute you saw his smiling face. But the most striking feature of Sonny Luongo was his remarkable, bright, deep, sky blue eyes.

Although Sonny Luongo was of Sicilian ancestry, with those attractive blue eyes there was clearly a sign that perhaps somewhere back in the ancient history of Sicily the Luongo family had been intertwined with the conquering Normans.

Mario Mastrano joined the army when he graduated high school in 1951. He did not go to Korea but was stationed in Germany for the three years that he was in the army. Mario felt kind of lucky that he did not see any action like Sonny did in Korea. Mario married a German girl while he was stationed in Germany. His family was not too pleased about him doing that because he got married in Germany and none of his family were able to attend his wedding. He has one son that is two years old.

Jackie looked at the pictures that Mario took out of his wallet and couldn't help but chuckle a little as he saw how short Mario's wife was standing next to him in the pictures. Mario was an inch or two taller than Jackie at a little over six feet tall. He was tall and thin, while his wife was lucky to be five feet tall.

Mario smiled and said to Jackie, "With her being so little it gives me more room in bed!"

Jimmy Valenti got married right after he graduated high school to his high school sweetheart, Sue Geronda. Jimmy had two children, two girls. The first girl was three years old and the second girl was a one-year-old. Jimmy's getting married kept him out of the service. Jimmy bought a house in Woburn, where he was living now. The guys gave him a hard time because Woburn has always been Winchester's arch rival in football and most everything else. There was always that stigma that Winchester had the rich kids and Woburn had the working class.

Jimmy was a pretty good football player. He was one of the linemen on the high school football team. Jimmy was always big, but since he got married he had put a little weight on. Jimmy gives his wife Sue credit for the extra pounds. "She is such a good cook," he admitted.

Bill Maggiori had rheumatic fever when he was a little kid. This caused him to have a slight heart murmur, which kept him out of the service. It also kind of stunted his growth a bit. Billy never got as tall or as big as the other guys. He admits that he keeps an eye on his health because he fears he might develop problems later in life from the rheumatic fever.

Bill works for his father's construction company as a project manager. Bill was not married, but he had been dating a girl from Medford for a couple of years now.

The guys had a couple of beers and caught up on old times and reminisced about growing up in the Village. Jackie asked how all the old characters from the neighborhood were doing, and he asked about a couple of old flames that he had dated in high school. The guys asked Jackie about his love life. He just alluded to enjoying the sun in Florida and how all of the girls have great tans. He mentioned that he spends a lot of time training but did have a couple of lady friends that he dated on occasion.

The guys gave Jackie a pretty good ribbing as they joked about the hotshot, good-looking pilot that was playing the field and having the time of his life. Jackie blushed a little and just smiled.

Jackie and the boys left the Sons of Italy Club around ten p.m. and traveled up to Green's Diner in Woburn for a cup of coffee. Green's Diner was right over the Winchester town line on Main Street in Woburn. It was a late night place where a lot of people would go for coffee and something to eat after being out for the evening.

Green's Diner was one of those old-fashioned diners that looked like a railroad train dining car, with stainless steel and bright green siding and big glass oval windows.

Jackie and the boys got a booth and had a cup of coffee and a piece of Green's famous apple pie. The place may have looked like a dive, but the food was pretty darn good. On a rare occasion my dad would treat Tony and me to breakfast if we were out early on a Saturday morning. Again, this was a very rare occurrence because the old man was really a little tight with his money.

Jackie and the boys left Green's around eleven p.m. Jackie drove the guys back to our house on the corner of Spruce and Oak as they all had their cars parked there.

Jackie thanked all the guys for getting together and having a nice night out. He promised to get together with them the next time he came home. Then he wished them all a very Merry Christmas.

They never mentioned Tommy Cantella, but they all knew that he was most likely up in heaven looking down on them and smiling. Tommy knows that he was the bond that kept them all together.

The North End

We were all up early as it was Friday, December 23. There was a definite air of anticipation and a feeling of Christmas as everyone sat down for breakfast.

Ma made French toast for breakfast. It was Friday, so we couldn't eat meat. We did not have the sausages Ma usually served with her French toast. My father only liked the fat Italian sausages, so that's the kind we got when Ma made sausages. I kind of liked the little link sausages, but we only got those when my father was not here for breakfast.

Gloria, Tony, and I were excited. We only had a half day of school and got out of class at 11:30 this morning. Ellen, Daddy, and Ma were getting out of work early today as well. Jackie mentioned that he was going into South Boston this morning to the Fargo Building to visit one of his college buddies, David Grady, who was also in the navy and was stationed at the Fargo Building, which was a naval administration building just outside of the South Boston Navy Yard. David was an Ensign and was assigned to recruiting and processing new navy recruits.

Jackie asked Tony and me, "Hey, you guys want to take a ride with me into the North End of Boston around noontime? I'm taking Aunty Sue and Aunty Laura into the North End to pick up the fish for the feast tomorrow night."

Both Tony and I gave a big yes to his invitation.

It was always a blast to go to the North End. This was the Italian section of Boston and was famous for its Italian delicacies. The North End was about as close as you can get to really being in Italy. The North End was very festive around Christmas time and would be fun to walk around.

Jackie told us, "Aunty Sue and Aunty Laura have the day off; they will be ready to go in town around noon, so you two guys meet me at Grandpa's house at noontime."

Aunty Sue and Aunty Laura always helped out with the Christmas feast. They were my mother's younger sisters, and neither one of them ever married. They had been taking care of Grandpa since Grammy died a few years ago.

Aunty Sue was a year younger than my mother. Like my mother she was on the short side. Actually, Aunty Sue was a couple of inches shorter than my mother. She stood just about five feet tall. She was somewhat petite and had very small features. Her mouth and lips were very small. As a matter of fact, she had told us that whenever she went to the dentist he complained about how small her mouth was and that it was hard for him to work on her teeth because of her small mouth. She had rosy cheeks, but I think that has more to do with the rouge she wore rather than her natural complexion. She had short, curly brown hair and a pretty smile.

Aunty Laura was exactly the same height as Aunty Sue. She was three years younger than my mother. Unlike Aunty Sue, Aunty Laura had round features. She had full, plump lips and a round face. She looked kind of like Grandpa only with more hair and no mustache. She was the youngest of the DeLuca girls and was in kind of a unique situation. She did not get involved with many family decisions. My mother and Aunty Sue seemed to take care of most details relating to Grandpa and family matters. Aunty Laura just seemed to be there to help take care of whatever my mother and Aunty Sue told her to do. She was not as serious as Aunty Sue and would always be ready to join us in playing games. She was a typical youngest child with a slight bit of mischief in her and a tendency to procrastinate when the opportunity arose.

My mother also had an older brother named Jimmy who owned a laundry in Somerville. We didn't see Uncle Jimmy that often, but he did stop by to see Grandpa and visit with us every once in a while. I guess Uncle Jimmy's wife had some kind of a disagreement with Grandpa, my mother, and the aunts, so he showed up alone when he came to visit. Aunty Sue and Aunty Laura were very close to our family, and along with Grandpa, they spent all of the holidays with us.

Actually their real names were not Sue and Laura. Aunty Sue's real name was Nunzia. She was named after the annunciation as she was born around the feast of the Annunciation, I was told. I guess this had something to do with when the angel Gabriel was sent by God to tell the Virgin Mary that she was with child. Anyway, when Aunty Sue started school at the old Chapin School on Swanton Street (which is not there anymore; I guess it caught fire and burned down a very long time ago) the teacher (who was not Italian) could not pronounce Nunzia, so she began calling her Sue.

The name has stuck with her since she was a child, so everyone called her Sue. Aunty Sue worked in the office at Schraft's candy factory in Sullivan Square in Charlestown.

Aunty Sue graduated from Winchester High School in 1923. Most women of her generation only went to the eighth grade for their education. Aunty Sue was very smart and continued school after the eighth grade. My mother and Aunty Laura only went to school until the eighth grade.

I don't quite understand Aunty Laura's situation. Her real name was Norma, but everyone called her Laura. I have to be honest; I was never told why she was called Laura not Norma. Actually I never asked why. Well, calling her Aunty Laura worked for me.

Aunty Laura also worked at Schraft's candy factory. Aunty Laura was a "dipper." All of the candy that Schraft's produced was hand dipped, which took a certain amount of skill.

We had been kind of spoiled by Aunty Sue and Aunty Laura. Most Friday nights they would bring home a ten-pound box of seconds. Seconds are the chocolates that did not get dipped properly and got pulled off of the production line and were sold at a discounted rate.

My favorites were the peppermint patties. I would go down the street to their house and watch television and sit there and eat peppermint patties like they were potato chips. Poor Grandpa couldn't eat the candy because he had sugar diabetes. I think he sneaked a few every once in a while though.

Aunty Sue checked Grandpa's sugar levels every Saturday morning. There was a certain process that she had to go through to check how his sugar levels were. Grandpa had to pee in a bottle on Saturday morning. Aunty Sue took some of the pee and put it in a test tube. She then heated a small pan of water and boiled it. She put the test tube in the boiling water and then added a couple of drops of something, I'm not sure what. If the pee turned blue, that meant Grandpa's sugar was okay. If the pee turned red when she put the drops in the tube, that meant that Grandpa's blood sugar level was high. They went through this process every Saturday morning.

Now I have a little secret to tell. When my mother went back to work at the laundry when I started school in kindergarten, after school, I would have to stay with Grandpa until my mother came home from work. He was supposed to watch me. I never figured out how an eighty-year-old guy with a wooden leg was supposed to watch an extremely active five-year-old. Heaven knows, if the house was on fire, Grandpa would have a hard time getting out.

When I got home from school I would come into the house and do the customary greeting, "Come sta il Papa-Nona?" He would give the standard "Medza medz."

After the greeting was over Grandpa would ask me in his broken English, "You gooda boy today?"

I would reply, "Yes, Grandpa."

Then he would pull out his little leather change purse that he kept in his sweater pocket. He would slowly open the change purse and pull out a nickel and say, "You gooda boy; I give you a cinque centesimi" (five cents).

Right up the street from Grandpa's house there was a corner store that sold penny candy. Believe me, for five cents you could get a whole bag of candy. Much of the candy was two for a penny.

I would look through the glass candy case with wide eyes as I picked my favorite pieces of candy; a Mary Jane, a mint julep, a piece of licorice, some chum gum (three for a penny, a real bargain), some wax lips, and a package of Smarties.

I would run home to Grandpa's house with my little paper bag full of candy. As soon as I walked through the door Grandpa would give me the ole "vieni qui piccino" (come here kid). He would say, "Whatsa you gut ina the bag?"

I would promptly turn the bag over to Grandpa. He would peruse the bag, giving it a determined scrutiny and nine out of ten times he would take the wax lips out of the bag and then nod to me with a gesture of Ima taka thisa one, and then he would smile.

The truth was that I actually bought the wax lips for Grandpa because I knew he liked them. He would break a piece of the wax candy off and chew it with a smile on his face.

As Grandpa spent quite a bit of time with me, he decided to teach me how to talk Italian. He began with some simple phrases and then taught me how to count to ten in Italian.

Teaching me to count to ten in Italian backfired on Grandpa because he would give me cinque centesimi (five cents) each day. I kind of figured out by counting in Italian that cinque meant five, so because I could count to ten now I knew that dieci meant ten.

So one day when Grandpa went through the ole "You gooda boy; I giva you cinque centesimi" routine, I replied, "Grandpa, how about giving me a dieci centesimi?"

With a huge smile on his face he laughed and said, "You shmartha boy!" He then started giving me a dime each day.

I loved going to Grandpa's house after school. He would always be good to me. He was alone all day, so he would kind of look forward to me coming over to his house.

Grandpa also taught me how to play Italian cards, although it got me in trouble with my friends. The game Grandpa taught me to play was like war only in Grandpa's game the jack would beat the queen.

Grandpa explained things to me as best he could. "In Italian cards the man is more powerful than the woman, so the jack beats the queen."

When I later played war with my buddies and they put a queen down and I put a jack down, I would take the cards figuring that I had won. I got an immediate, "Hey, what are you doing?"

"The queen beats the jack!" they would say.

I would reply, "Not according to my grandfather."

I was rudely told, "Well, when you play cards with your grandfather you can play that the jack beats the queen, but in our game the queen beats the jack!"

When Aunty Sue, who sometimes had a tendency to be a little bossy, would come home from work, she would walk in the door and immediately ask Grandpa all sorts of questions. He would grumble and mumble under his breath. You could tell Grandpa would start to get irritated just before Aunty Sue would come home at around 4:30 p.m. each night.

I thought it always kind of funny that both Aunty Sue and Aunty Laura were lucky to be five feet tall, but in Aunty Sue's case she was a little spitfire the way she handed out orders. You would think that she was seven feet tall the way she bossed Grandpa and Aunty Laura around.

Tony and I would see Aunty Sue in action and mumble under our breath that we should be calling her Uncle Suzy!

One afternoon at about three p.m. Grandpa got up from his chair, got his crutches, and slowly moved toward the basement door. He then gave me a, "Vieni qui."

I hustled over to the basement door. He opened the door and gestured for me to stand on the step below him. He put his hand firmly on my shoulder as we made our way step by step down the cellar stairs. When we got to the bottom of the stairs, we made our way over to the wine cellar where Grandpa kept the homemade wine that he would make each fall.

Grandpa had two stools in the room with the wine barrels, a little stool and a bigger stool. He also had two glasses in the room, a regular glass (the kind that jelly came in) and a whiskey shot glass. Grandpa sat down on the big stool, and he gestured for me to sit on the little stool.

Grandpa would then open the spigot and pour himself a glass of wine in the regular wine glass, and then he took the shot glass and filled it up and gave it to me. He proceeded to do this two more times. However, I was limited to the one shot. He then wiped his mustache and got up from the stool. We made our way back upstairs, and he was back in his chair just before Aunty Sue walked through the door.

When Aunty Sue curtly asked, "Pa, how are you doing today?"

Grandpa, with a smile on his face, replied, "Ima justa fine."

I would go home from Grandpa's house with a smile on my face as well.

Ma would ask me, "What did you and Grandpa do today?"

I would reply, "We just had fun together."

My mother and the rest of my family could not understand why a little boy would enjoy being with such an old man.

This little venture to the wine cellar became a daily event until I had to take over the paper route for Tony. I felt bad that Grandpa couldn't go down cellar for his little dose of happiness anymore. But now maybe his blood sugar might improve.

Tony and I showed up at Grandpa's house just before noon. Jackie's car was parked out front. Tony didn't have basketball practice that afternoon, but he had taken a part-time job sweeping the floors at the hardware store up the street from our house. Mr. Bavuso told Tony he could show up when he had the time and sweep the floors and take the trash out.

It was nice of Mr. Bavuso to give Tony this job. It gave Tony some spending money, and his hours were flexible. I had the big day. It was collection day and this was the last collection day before Christmas, so this was going to be the big payday!

Tony and I went inside to say hello to Grandpa. He was always happy to see his grandchildren. Jackie was having a cup of tea and some little sandwiches with Aunty Sue and Aunty Laura.

Jackie told Tony and me, "We will be leaving in just a minute."

Tony and I both mentioned to Jackie that we had to be home around 3:15 p.m. He told us that should not be a problem as long as we didn't hit too much traffic in downtown Boston.

Jackie knew I had to meet the 3:45 p.m. train from Boston to pick up the late edition of The Record American. He also knew that today was my big payday.

Jackie let me know, "Billy, I can't drive you around the paper route today 'cause I have to pick up Ma when we get back and take her to Medford Square."

I told him, "That's okay. I'm used to walking the route, but I do appreciate your help the past couple of days"

Aunty Sue sat in the front seat, and Aunty Laura, Tony, and I sat in the backseat of Jackie's car. It had gotten really cold, and it looked like it was going to snow again. Jackie took South Border Road through the woods to get to the Mystic Valley Park Way for us to get into Boston.

We traveled past the army camp on South Border Road that was on the Winchester,-Medford town line. We saw all of the Army trucks and jeeps lined up near the front gate of the camp. They looked like toys the way they were parked right inside of the entrance to the camp.

We got to the end of South Border Road and got on the parkway. The street cars ran down the middle of the road between the north and south sides of the road. Jackie got beside one of the trolleys, and it looked like they were having a race as we drove down the Parkway.

We got to Wellington Circle and the Trolley took a left toward Everett. We went over the bridge that crossed the Mystic River that divided Medford and Somerville. We took a left and went past the new Edsel plant. It was so interesting to watch them making the cars. You could see right through the big windows and could watch the assembly line from the street.

The Edsel plant had just recently opened. It was manufacturing the first model year of the Edsel. The Edsel was scheduled to be unveiled to the public on September 4, 1957. We couldn't see the finished product, but you could see the various parts of the car as they rolled by on the assembly line. There was a lot of talk about Ford choosing Somerville to put the new Edsel plant. My dad said, "Building the Edsel in Somerville will provide lots of jobs for years to come." I guess that's a good thing if you needed a job.

Aunty Sue and Aunty Laura both let Tony and me know just when we were going by the Schraft's candy factory. Sometimes I wonder if they thought we were blind and couldn't see the giant building with the big huge sign on top of it that was lighted in red letters that spelled Schraft's.

Boston was such a busy place. We crossed the North Washington Street Bridge and hit the intersection next to the Boston Garden. Jackie turned left down Commercial Street and then took a right onto Hanover Street.

Sometimes when I sat with Grandpa and he was listening to Signora Blanco on the Italian radio station, I heard the announcer rattle off this quick flurry of Italian words that sounded like blah, blah blah blah, and then I would hear very clearly Hanover Street, and then the announcer went back to talking in Italian.

Jackie was lucky. Here it was one of the busiest shopping days in the North End, and Jackie had found a parking spot on Hanover Street not too far from Parmenter Street. Jufree's Fish Market was actually on Salem Street, but we had to walk down Parmenter Street to get to Salem Street.

Jackie helped Aunty Sue and Aunty Laura out of the car. Tony and I couldn't believe all the activity that was going on in the North End. There were Christmas lights in every window. The snow that was piled up on the edges of the sidewalks looked almost gray from all the soot and traffic in the city. But the wonder of it all was the stores and shops that we were passing by.

The best way to describe what we were seeing would be to say that we were in the zoo, but all the animals were dead and hanging on a hook, in front of all the stores.

On one side of the street there was a goat, a pig, rabbits, lots of rabbits actually, and a lamb. On the other side of the street there were chickens, geese, ducks, and turkeys hanging on hooks. This was wild!

All of the animals had their feathers and fur, and the spooky part was that all of them had their eyes open! It was like they were looking right through you.

We worked our way down Parmenter Street to Salem Street. Polcari's Coffee Shop was on the corner. The smells were wild in there; you picked up the scent of the chestnut vendors that were roasting chestnuts over a bed of charcoals along with dead animals, fish, and coffee.

When you enter Jufree's Fish Market you got hit with the smell of fish, fish, and more fish.

Aunty Sue had a list with her. She needed to pick up five live eels, three pounds of smelts, a couple of pounds of baccala, some scongeli, some calamari, a couple of lobsters, and some clams—actually, she was getting quahogs, which were really big clams.

Jufree's was packed with everyone getting their fish for the feast of the seven fishes. We finally got a guy to come over and help us. He took us over to the barrel that had the live eels in it. This was great! It looked like hundreds of black snakes were swimming around in the barrel.

I couldn't believe that this guy was just sticking his hand in the barrel and taking out eels. The eel was wrapping itself around the guys arm. Aunty Sue wanted to make sure that they were lively and pretty good sized.

Grandpa called the eels the cubathona. He loved eating them. I was not a big fan of the eels, but I always had to have a little bit because it's kind of a good luck tradition on Christmas Eve.

The guy put the eels in a bucket with a top on it so they wouldn't escape.

Now we were getting the lobsters, two good-sized ones about two pounds each. They were squirming and waving their claws all over the place. It's a good thing that the claws had those rubber bands on them. I bet their claw could take your finger right off.

The guy that was helping us did not speak English very well, so Aunty Sue was talking to him in Italian. Jackie and Tony were scoping out the quahogs and making sure that they were big enough for Ma to stuff. Jackie and Tony loved Ma's stuffed quahogs.

Aunty Laura, who brought the pocketbook with the money in it, was clutching her handbag close to her bosom. She wanted to make sure because it was so crowded in the store that no one ran off with her pocketbook.

At long last Aunty Sue had all of her items. Aunty Laura asked, "How much did everything cost?"

Aunty Laura took out a bunch of crisp new bills. You would almost think that she just printed them in Grandpa's basement.

As we left Jufree's Fish Market it began to snow lightly. The snow looked so pretty coming down around all the lights and wreaths that were hanging on each lamppost. On our way back to the car Aunty Sue wanted to stop to pick up some fresh fruit at the fruit stand. Aunty Sue was mesmerized by the sight of the navel oranges on the fruit stand. Oranges were hard to come by in Boston in December.

Jackie laughed as he told Aunty Sue, "For mile upon mile on the roads in Florida all you ever see are orange trees filled with oranges. I will send you some oranges when I get back to Florida."

Aunty Sue stopped and picked up some fresh fruit and some mixed nuts anyway. "With all the company we will be getting during the holidays I'm sure that we will need everything," she lets us all know.

As we walked back to Jackie's car we passed another chestnut vendor. Jackie turned to Tony and me and said, "Hey, you guys want to try a couple of roasted chestnuts."

They smelled so good that we both smiled and said, "Sure."

Jackie picked up a small bag and handed them to Tony. They were warm and oh so tasty. A nice little treat!

We were all loaded up with various types of fish, fruit, and nuts. Jackie was pretty brave to be putting this stuff in the trunk of his brand new car!

We got to the car just at 2:30 p.m. With any kind of luck we would be home by 3:15 p.m. Jackie turned the car around and headed back down Hanover Street to Commercial Street. He took a left and slowly edged his way into the traffic.

It was snowing a little more now. As we approached the intersection with the elevated tracks where the elevated train turns to cross the North Washington Street Bridge, we were stopped by the Boston policeman that was standing in the middle of the intersection directing traffic. He was all bundled up with his long blue topcoat with the brass buttons and a pair of white mittens.

As Jackie came to a stop in the front of the line of traffic, with his blinker signaling a right hand turn, the big cop in the middle of the street gave Jackie a growl and told him, "Pull over to the side of the road."

It was cold and snowing, and now this guy pulled Jackie over. There was a bit of concern on everyone's face that was in the car. Aunty Sue had this look on her face that would normally signal an immediate bowel movement would be needed! A mixture of pain and anticipation, or maybe I should really say constipation?

The big Boston cop stopped all the traffic and lumbered over toward Jackie's car. Jackie pushed the button for the automatic window. The window zipped down, which allowed a blast of cold air and snow to come into the car.

Jackie was cool as a cucumber as the police man leaned down and looked into Jackie's face and then he blurted out, "Are you crazy?"

Now Jackie had a puzzled look on his face.

The big Boston cop cracked a huge smile and said, "Hey buddy, you must be crazy if you're from Florida, and you're here in Boston in this kind of weather."

At this point, Jackie started laughing out loud. The policeman said, "I saw your Florida license plate and figured I just had to give you a hard time."

The traffic had become all backed up and people were starting to beep their horns. The policeman took his big white mitten off and shook Jackie's hand and wished him a Merry Christmas and a safe trip back to Florida.

Jackie closed the window and took the right hand turn heading over the bridge; everyone in the car breathed a big sigh of relieve and let out a big laugh. Actually we laughed about the policeman all the way home!

The Big Payday

Jackie drove to our house on Oak Street to drop off the fish and all the stuff that the aunts bought in the North End.

The aunts told Jackie, "We are going to start some of the preparation this afternoon for the feast tomorrow. We will be helping your mother to cook all of the fish and the other dishes."

Although neither one of the aunts were married, Aunty Sue had been cooking the meals for her, Aunty Laura, and Grandpa. Aunty Sue had actually become a very good cook. I may be creating a little controversy here, but there were some dishes that Aunty Sue made that were as good as, if not better than, my mom made. This may be considered heresy in the Shields family as Ma was considered the head chef and culinary expert of the family. Don't get me wrong; she was a fabulous cook, but Aunty Sue did have her moments.

The aunts start to go into the house just as my mother was coming out. They talked for a minute because my mother had to give them some direction on what to do. Being the older sister and the matriarch of the family, my mother would be the maestro of the feast, giving directions as if she was conducting a symphony.

Ma gave the aunts their marching orders and then headed out to meet Jackie so that he could take her to Medford for some last-minute shopping.

Tony headed off to the hardware store to sweep the floors, and I grabbed my canvas Boston Globe newspaper sack and headed down to the news store.

It may have been cold and snowing lightly, but deep down inside me I had a warm glow along with a skip in my step and a smile on my face because today was collection day.

It's funny how motivation and anticipation could change your whole outlook on things. I guess it's kind of like what my father had always been preaching to us kids: Life is what you make it; if you want your life to be miserable, it will; if you want your life to be happy, it will.

The old man had always been very philosophical. He was always coming up with witty comments and anecdotes. Another one of his words of wisdom would be: If you really want to do something, you'll find a way: if you don't, you'll find an excuse.

Well, no excuses for me. I was very motivated and looking forward to the rewards of the day.

I walked into the newspaper barn, and I couldn't believe it, Mr. Mullen was playing Christmas music. And he had on a Santa hat. If I didn't know better I would think that old Mr. Mullen snuck into Grandpa's homemade wine!

I loved Christmas music; I often practiced being a disc jockey with my records when I was all alone in my room. I had a collection of Christmas records that I played on the record player that my sister Ellen gave to me on my birthday last year.

My favorite was Gene Autry's "Rudolph the Red-Nosed Reindeer," and I even like the flip side, "If it Doesn't Snow on Christmas." My other favorites were: "Frosty the Snowman," "White Christmas," "I'll be Home for Christmas," "Joy to the World," and of course, "Angels We Have Heard on High." After all they sing about my sister Gloria in that song!

Jackie told me, "When I was driving home from Florida I had the radio on and they must have played the song 'I'll be Home for Christmas' a hundred times. It made me feel good that I would actually be home for Christmas this year."

Jackie was telling Dad that he might be leaving on a cruise to the Far East on the aircraft carrier The Hancock sometime in the late spring or early summer of 1957, and that he would probably not make it home for Christmas next year because the cruise was scheduled for at least seven months. So as the song said, "I'll be home for Christmas, if only in my dreams," might be a possibility for Jackie next year.

"Hey Shieldsy, you need a hand getting the late edition at the train station this afternoon?" Would wonders ever cease? Charlie Vassali was actually asking me if he could help me with the papers!

I never thought I'd see the day that Charlie Vassali would be offering me help. Perhaps it had to do with me letting Charlie use my sled yesterday. Dividends already from my new sled!

"Nah, I'm all set, Charlie, but thanks for offering," I quickly replied to Charlie.

"No problem," Charlie said with a smile.

"Hey, it's snowing again; maybe we will be able to go sledding tomorrow. It sure was fun sledding at Lincoln School hill yesterday," Charlie reminded me.

"Maybe we will, but tomorrow was a busy day. I have to do my Christmas shopping in the morning, and then there's the feast tomorrow night," I told Charlie.

"Yeah, my mother has been getting things ready all day today for the big fish feast," Charlie replied.

"It's not a fish feast; it's the Feast of the Seven Fishes," I let him know, with an air of authority.

"Hey, you are right; Christmas wouldn't be the same for us Italians if we didn't do the Feast of the Seven Fishes on Christmas," Charlie sheepishly acknowledged.

I couldn't believe that I was actually having a real conversation with Charlie Vassali, and he was actually calling me Billy rather than the foul names that he usually called me.

Ahh, the spirit of Christmas at work. What's next; was old man Mullen going to give me a bag full of nickels or something?

Well, I should enjoy the moment; I'm sure things will be back to normal real soon, and Charlie would be giving me a wedgie or noogies on the head or something like that and calling me the usual pet names he has for me.

I grabbed the two-wheel dolly and headed for the train station; it was almost quarter to four, and Mr. Bagely and the papers would be there soon.

I had to push the two-wheel dolly down the middle of Thompson Street because the snow from the storm a couple of days ago was all packed up around the edge of the sidewalks and there were so many people out shopping that the sidewalks on both sides of the street were really crowded. I didn't want to push anyone over, so I just walked down the street.

With all the cars parked on both sides of the street, the mounds of snow had it so the cars couldn't get close to the curb, so the street was really narrow. Thompson Street had all these little shops on it, and there were Christmas shoppers everywhere. You could really tell it was almost Christmas. All of the shops had Christmas lights strung up around the doors and windows and every lamppost had a Christmas wreath on it. As I walked down the street with the snow lightly falling, I almost felt like I was walking in a Currier and Ives painting.

As I passed by the post office at the end of Thompson Street I could see lots of people carrying bundles and packages to and from the entrance to the post office. Even the post office had lights strung up around the entrance.

Oh jeez, I see the headlight of the train coming down the track from Wedgemere station! I couldn't believe the train was on time.

The ramp up to the train was a little slippery, so I would have to remember to be careful as I pushed the dolly down the ramp on my way back to the paper store. I did not want to take a header and get injured.

The bell clanging on the train as it pulled into the train station almost sounded like it was playing a Christmas tune of some kind. It was just starting to get dark, but I could see Mr. Bagely waving as the train slowly came to a stop.

"Hey there, Billy, a very merry Christmas to you this afternoon," Mr. Bagely shouted to me in a loud voice as the train came to a stop.

"A very merry Christmas to you as well," I shouted back to him.

"It sure is another cold one today," Mr. Bagely shouted as he put the ramp down and handed me the papers. "The papers are small today," he added as he helped me put them on the two-wheel dolly.

"Yeah, the papers will be easy to carry around on my route today," I replied.

"Well, you and your family have a wonderful Christmas," Mr. Bagely said as he held his hand out to help a lady as she started down the stairs of the train.

As I started to push the dolly I turned to Mr. Bagely and said to him, "Hey, Mr. Bagely, thanks for all your help with the papers. I really appreciate it, and a very merry Christmas to you and your family as well!"

I remembered to push the dolly down the ramp very slowly. It was becoming kind of slippery from the snow. I headed up Thompson Street with a big smile on my face. I was about to begin my quest for wealth and fame. Well, hopefully wealth, I wasn't sure about the fame.

All of the paperboys were waiting at the end of the alley that headed back to the newspaper shack. "Hey,

Shields, it took you long enough to get here," Charlie Vassali shouted with a look of anger and aggravation on his face.

Hmm, back to his old self again. Well, that spurt of Christmas kindness sure didn't last very long.

Mr. Mullen's son Seamus doled out the late edition of The Record American to the anxiously awaiting paperboys. I swear he was taking his time on purpose just to aggravate everyone.

As I finished loading the last of my newspapers in my canvas paper sack, Seamus barked out to all the paperboys, "You guys be smart and treat the customers right today."

It amazed me how grownups expect perfection from kids when few of them can get through a day without screwing something up.

I slung the sack of newspapers over my shoulder and adjusted the load and then started my trek toward Shore Road.

The walk up Shore Road seemed like it would take forever. I understood why they say good things come to those who wait, but I must admit I was born impatient and was always in a hurry to get my just reward.

I finally had Mrs. Napoli's house in sight. Her house looked like Fort Knox this afternoon. The windfall was about to start. I dropped the sack of newspapers at the end of the walk and with a skip in my step I quickly climbed the stairs and knocked on the door of my first customer of the day. Oh boy, I was getting really excited. I better control myself and not look too anxious.

Mrs. Napoli opened the door and my nose immediately got a blast of the smell of fish frying. I had to hold my breath for a second so she wouldn't see me gagging from the putrid smell. Geez, what was she cooking, skunk fish?

Mrs. Napoli was always cooking something; she had a big family, and they all liked to eat. I think Mrs. Napoli kind of cheated a little when she was preparing the family meals. She might be testing the food and sampling her cooking a little too much.

If Mrs. Napoli was ever kidnapped and the police asked me to describe what she looked like, I would have to say a bowling ball with arms!

I handed the Boston Globe to Mrs. Napoli; she gave me the normal forty-five cents that she gave me every week, which was five cents a day for the globe and ten cents for the Winchester Star on Thursdays and a five cent tip. Then she smiled and said, "Hold on a minute, Billy; I've got something for you."

Ahh, the first of my many pay-offs, I thought to myself. Then she handed me a box that was wrapped with the ugliest Christmas wrapping paper I'd ever seen.

She added, "I do hope that you enjoy your gift. You and your family have a Merry Christmas." Then she closed the door.

I quickly walked back down the steps and immediately began to open the box with great anticipation. I got the ugly wrapping paper off and took the cover off the box. I just stared at what was in the box.

"You've got to be kidding me," I shouted out loud. A tie, a friggin' tie! Who gives a ten year old kid a friggin' tie? And an ugly one at that, red and blue polka dots with a green background. What the heck was I going to do with this; wear a clown suit with a big red nose and huge floppy shoes when I wore the tie?

"This is not a good sign, definitely not a good sign," I grumbled to myself. "If this is what happens with the rest of the customers, I swear I'll jump head first off the Shore Road Bridge and into the icy Aberjona River!"

Oh, well. Maybe there won't be fame and fortune after all.

As I hustled off to my next stop a light bulb suddenly went off in my head, and I had this brilliant idea. I know what I'd do. I'd do the exact same thing that Mrs. Napoli probably did. I'll re-gift the tie and give it to my brother Tony for Christmas! This way it would save me some money, and I could get rid of the ugly tie. See, I guess maybe there was a silver lining to every cloud.

Thank heavens the rest of my customers on Spruce Street were not like Mrs. Napoli. I did well on Spruce Street thanks to the generosity of my DeLuca cousins. I did have a bunch of them in the Spruce Street neighborhood, and they always treated me right.

I worked my way up Spruce Street and on to the bottom of Swanton Street. I had delivered nineteen papers and had forty-one more to deliver. So far I'd gotten twenty-one dollars and fifty-five cents in tips and one stupid tie!

I had a total of sixty customers; forty-one took The Boston Globe, eleven took The Record American, eight took The Herald, and one took The Christian

Science Monitor. I had twenty-eight customers that took The Winchester Star on Thursdays.

The daily newspaper cost five cents. Of that five cents I got one penny for each paper that I delivered. The Winchester Star costs ten cents and only comes out on Thursday night. I got two cents for delivering the Winchester Star. With sixty customers that took the paper six days a week that would be three dollars and sixty cents. Twenty-eight Winchester Stars at two cents each equals fifty-six cents, for a total of four dollars and eighteen cents a week plus tips. I averaged just about a ten cents a week tip from each customer, which would give me a grand total of ten dollars, give or take a few cents, each week.

Of the ten dollars I made, I usually turned six dollars over to Ma for the house. All of us kids had been contributing to the house since we got jobs. Ma said that we needed to share to make ends meet. I had this mental picture of Ma stretching a dollar bill into a big circle until both ends met.

My paper route went up and down Spruce Street to Swanton Street, where I turned right up the hill past Angie's pastry store. I had a couple of customers in Quigley Court, which was off of Swanton Street, and a couple of customers on Emerson Court, which was also off of Swanton Street. I continued past Neno's Market and took a left onto Chester Street. I went down Chester and took a left onto Raymond Place, where I had the one customer that took The Christian Science Monitor. I then took a left onto Florence Street and headed back toward Swanton Street. I then crossed Swanton and headed down Holland Street, where I took a right onto Oak Street and finish up at my house.

At different times of the year the amount of customers would go up and down, but it always stayed around sixty.

I had to admit I persevered the past few months and made it through the fish smells and growling dogs, which had allowed me to finish the year with a very good Christmas haul.

I had been trying to keep a running count as I left each house; however, I lost count when Mrs. Suldeno on Swanton Street gave me a handful of change. I did not want to be rude and count the change in front of her so I just shoved it in my pocket and said thank you and got out of her kitchen before the smell of fried haddock and garlic got to me. I would count my winnings when I got home.

With the last paper delivered and no late edition tomorrow night because it was Christmas Eve, my work was done for a couple of days. I was just going to enjoy the family and the Christmas season and spend as much time as I could with Jackie.

Our house at the corner of Spruce and Oak Streets looked pretty good as I walked down Holland Street. It seemed that Dad did an extra special job this year putting the Christmas lights up around the front porch. He even wrapped lights around the columns, a nice touch!

It stopped snowing, which was good. We only got a dusting, so we would not have to shovel. The fresh snow looked great as it covered the gray and tinged snow around the edges of the street that were made dirty from the exhaust smoke of the cars and trucks that passed by. The fresh covering of snow and all the Christmas lights in the neighborhood sure did make it look a lot like Christmas.

As I approached the driveway and the backyard I saw that both Dad's and Jackie's cars were parked there. Hopefully Ma and her assistant Gloria had cooked up something special. Tomorrow night was the big Feast of The Seven Fishes, and since it was Friday night, we couldn't eat meat, I was wondering what might be on the menu. I'd soon find out.

As I walked through the back door into the kitchen, I got hit with the most wonderful smell of all: pizza!

This was fantastic! Ma was making homemade pizza. The aroma of the pizza baking in the oven smelled wonderful. I was almost as if my nose was full of little Italian pizza makers doing a tarantella in there and waving little pizzas all around as they danced and sprinkling basil and oregano like confetti.

I got a full reception from the family; first Jackie, who was playing pinochle with Dad, gave me a, "Hey, Billy, how did you do? Should we call the Brinks truck to take you down to the paper store?"

Then I got a big smile and a hug from Ma, whose hands were all full of white flour.

Gloria gave me a, "Hey, Chicken Bones, is it still snowing out?"

And my father gave me a wink and a, "It's nice to have you home, Billy."

Dad added, "Tony and Ellen are upstairs. Would you please let them know that you are home and that they should come downstairs for supper?"

I ran upstairs and let Tony and Ellen know that I was home. I then ran into my room and emptied my pockets on the bed. There were so many dollar bills and a ton of coins.

I made a quick tally of the bills and come up with $68.00. This included one-dollar bills and a couple of five-dollar bills. I stacked the quarters in fours and came up with $12.25 in quarters. I counted the rest of the dimes nickels and pennies and wound up with a grand total of $88.93.

I got a pencil and paper and wrote down $88.93 and then subtracted $20.80, which was the cost of the papers for the week. This came to $68.13, but I had to add in my commission for selling the papers, which was a penny a paper a day for the Globe, Record American and Herald. Then there was the two cents a paper for The Winchester Star. This came to $4.18. Oh yeah, I forgot the five cents for The Christian Science Monitor. That made the total $4.23. Now I had to add the $4.23 to the $68.13, which made a grand total of $72.36. Wow, I was rich!

I would tuck the money away in the bottom drawer of my bureau until tomorrow morning when I had to cash out with Mr. Mullen for the week at the paper store.

Earlier this afternoon Ma sent Tony next door to Marino's bakery to get some bread dough so that she could make pizza for tonight's supper. Even though she had all that work to do for tomorrow's Feast of the Seven Fishes, she still came up with a whopper of a meal.

Ma did a great job of whipping up a couple of pizza pies. Actually she made three of them, one with just scamorza cheese, another with anchovies, and another with peppers, mushrooms, and onions. They all had cheese on them and that zesty tomato sauce that Ma concocted along with the toppings.

Meal time was always interesting at the Shields house. It seemed that everyone had something to contribute to the conversation. Dad had always encouraged us to share the events of the day with one another. It was therapeutic to express your thoughts and feelings and to know that the people you are sharing with really cared about you.

I felt that for me, meal time enhanced my education, especially about my own family. Dad had shared his experience and adventures from the time he spent in the Aleutian Islands in Alaska during World War Two and the work he was involved with on a daily basis in the navy yard.

Ma was always telling us about the people she worked with at the laundry and about her time growing up with her family.

Ellen always had a story about the telephone company and working in Boston. Gloria, Tony, and I discussed our days at school and our friends, and with Jackie home and having meals with us for the past few days, it had been really enlightening to learn about jet airplanes and Florida and the many adventures and activities that Jackie was involved with. As I said, we shared, we laughed, we teased, but most of all we loved.

As Dad always said, "Without family you have nothing."

From what we had gathered over the years, Dad did not have much of a family life growing up in Wilkes Barre, Pennsylvania. So I guess he was trying to make up for it by instilling true family values in his children. He was always preaching, "Get along with one another, and remember in the whole scheme of things, when it comes right down to it, the only ones that you can truly count on in life are your family."

Unlike the Italian pizzeria that used round pans, Ma used square pans to make her pizza. It was a little thicker than the kind we got at DePasqualie's Pizzeria in South Medford the once a year Aunty Sue took us there. We had found that eating out at a restaurant like DePasqualie's was a luxury that most families in the village couldn't afford. I thought Ma made a better pizza anyway!

We sat, ate, talked, and laughed as we immensely enjoyed the time we spent simply eating a pizza pie together. Jackie and Dad had a Carlings beer, Ma and Ellen had a glass of wine, and Tony, Gloria, and I had orange soda.

Life sure was good, and this particular day it did not seem like it could get any better!

Christmas Eve

It was great to sleep a little late. It was Saturday, so everyone got to sleep a little later than usual. I rubbed the sleep from eyes and jumped out of bed. I was happy to see that the sun was out. It had been cloudy and snowy for a couple of days, which made it real Christmassy and all, but it was nice to see the sun shining.

I ran to the bathroom, but the door was closed. I'm not sure who was in there, but I did pick up the scent of gold Dial soap coming through the door, which usually meant it would be Jackie. He was the only one that used Dial gold. It had a unique smell that was a very clean smell. Ma always bought Palmolive soap. Jackie carried his own Dial gold in his travel bag.

I ran downstairs to the other bathroom. I turned the corner at the bottom of the stairs and cut through the parlor and entered the kitchen. Dad was sitting at the table in his usual spot at the head of the table, with his back to the wall so he could look out at all parts of the room. He was reading the paper, and Ma was, where else, at the stove cooking breakfast.

I gave them my standard morning greeting: "Good morning, how are you two this morning?"

I got a warm, "Good morning. Are you excited? Today is Christmas Eve," (like I really needed to be reminded) from my mom.

Dad looked over the newspaper with his glasses pushed down over his nose and gave me a, "Top of the morning there, Billy boy."

I hightailed it to the bathroom, and when I was done I headed back upstairs to get dressed for the day. I had much to do this day. I had to do my turn-ins at the paper store and settle up with Mr. Mullen. Then it was over to F.W. Woolworth's to do my Christmas shopping. Next I had to come home and wrap all of the presents that I bought.

The first order of business for the day was to have breakfast. I did not catch what Ma was putting together when I said good morning. I was in too much of a rush to get to the bathroom. Knowing Ma it would be something really good.

I quickly got dressed and headed back downstairs. I entered the kitchen and found everyone there, as if they magically appeared. Five minutes ago no one was in the kitchen but Ma and Daddy, now everyone was sitting at the table.

You could tell that it was Saturday morning. Ellen had on a pair of khaki slacks, a pink sweater, and a pair of white sneakers with bobby socks. She surely was not dressed for work today. Gloria could barely keep her eyes open. I swear she only got out of bed because Ma told her to come down for breakfast. She still had her pajamas on as she sat at the table half asleep. Tony and Jackie both look liked they are ready to go chop wood. The two of them had on plaid shirts and jeans.

I finally figured out what Ma was making for breakfast and knew why they all assembled so quickly. She was making zeppelis (fried dough), an all-time favorite in our house.

Apparently Ma had some leftover bread dough from last night's pizzas, so she decided to make us fried dough for breakfast. This was a great treat!

Perhaps because Jackie was home, I'm not sure, but Ma had pulled out all the stops with regard to the cuisine she had been preparing of late. The fried dough, which we call zeppelis, was served but a few times a year. They are very rich and sweet, so it's best if the body does not get too much of them, so I'm told. Heck, I'd eat them every day if I could!

I was watching Ma make the zeppelis. She made it look simple. First she puts a big frying pan on the stove and puts about an inch of oil in the pan. She gets the oil relatively hot but not too hot. Then she takes the pound of bread dough and stretches it into a long thin rolls, kind of like the shape of a rolling pin. Then she cuts off little pieces that are about the size of a golf ball.

She proceeds to stretch the ball of dough so that it is like a little pizza, real thin and about six inches around. As the oil was now at the right temperature, she placed the little round pizza-shaped piece of dough in the frying pan. It cooks real fast; it kind of puffs up and gets real fluffy. She flips it once and cooks it on both sides

When it's golden brown on both sides, she takes it from the pan and puts it on a couple of napkins and lets the excess oil drain from the dough as it cools.

Now the fun part comes. You get to sprinkle whatever you like onto the piece of hot dough. The choices are confectionary sugar (the white powdery kind), regular sugar, and maybe some cinnamon or some brown sugar (the kind of sugar with molasses in it). You can also spread butter on the hot dough and add some jelly.

Ma put a jar of her blueberry jelly on the table. Or you could be like my goofy brother Tony and put peanut butter on the fried dough (Yuk! what a waste of good fried dough). No matter what you choose, it's really good!

Dad had the radio on and they were playing Christmas songs on WCOP. All of a sudden the song, "I'm Getting Nuttin' for Christmas" came on the radio. You would think that the Shields family was trying out for the Mitch Miller chorus the way they all chimed in and sang the song, and as they were singing they all pointed at me and started laughing hysterically.

"Hey, Billy, is this your song." Gloria giggled.

The abuse that a ten-year-old has to take from his family is just not fair!

"I'm glad that I can provide so much amusement for the family," I replied to them all with a smile on my face. "Good thing I know that you guys are kidding me," I tell them, "because I'm about to go Christmas shopping. Someone with a lesser nature than I have just might decide to go to Symmes Grain and Feed Store and get all of you a bag of coal for Christmas!"

The back doorbell rang; it was Steve and Bobby. They were coming downtown with me to do Christmas shopping. Steve and Bobby came into the kitchen and said good morning to everyone. Ma offered them some fried dough, but they both declined politely saying that they had breakfast already.

I let everyone know that I was going downtown to turn in for the week at the paper store, and then I was going to do my Christmas shopping at F.W. Woolworth's.

Ellen reminded me, "Say hello to Vera Vassali for me." Yes, Charlie Vassali's sister who works at F.W. Woolworth's.

I let Ellen know, "I'll say hello."

Jackie looked over at us and said, "Hey guys, I'll give you a ride downtown. I have to go out and pick up some pastry for Ma."

Steve's and Bobby's eyes lit up. They would gladly jump at the chance to ride in Jackie's new Mercury Monterey.

After looking at Steve and Bobby, I gave Jackie the answer that they want me to give. "Sure, we would love a ride downtown."

I was just about to leave, when Ma decided she had to give me instructions before I left. "First of all, be careful with all the money you have with you." Then she told me, "Do not to spend your money foolishly on Christmas presents and do not buy things that people don't need."

Geez, I thought to myself, but grown-ups sure know how to put a chill on the holiday festivities!

I assured Ma, "I will be careful with my money and only buy good things for people." Then I let Jackie know, "We will be outside in the car waiting for you."

Steve, Bobby, and I scooted out the back door as Jackie was being given last-minute directions from Ma on what kind of pastry to pick up at Angie's pastry store. We always got lots of visitors on Christmas Day, so Ma wanted to make sure she had plenty of pastry on hand when the people showed up.

We headed toward Jackie's car. I opened the door and held the seat back so that Steve and Bobby can get in the backseat. After all, I got shotgun.

Jackie came out of the house with a smile on his face as he jumped in the car and started it up. He gave me a rub on the head and told me, "When you turn in your money this morning make sure that when Mr. Mullen is counting the quarters he doesn't use the ole three finger trick."

This was something that no one has been able to actually prove, but we just know it happens. It happened when he was counting the quarters two by two with his fingers, he sometimes slips a third finger in there when you're not looking and cheats you out of a quarter as he takes three quarters but only credits you for two.

I let Jackie know, "Don't worry, I will be watching for the ole three finger trick."

It was a beautiful day outside. Cool but not bitterly cold, and it was sunny, which made it really bright because the sun was reflecting off of the white snow on the ground. The ride downtown was short but enjoyable.

Jackie dropped us off in front of the paper store. Steve, Bobby, and I headed down the alley to the shack in the back of the store. Mr. Mullen and his two boys had on Santa hats again. What an oxymoron, the Mullen guys wearing Santa caps. That's kind of like the Grim Reaper wearing a baptism outfit.

I was happy to see that Eddie Quinn was handling the turn-ins today. With Eddie counting the money I could rest assured that he would not cheat me. Eddie was a stand-up guy who kind of watched out for us kids. I often wondered how such a nice guy like Eddie got tied up with the Mullens. I heard that Eddie served in the army with Mr. Mullen in the Second World War, and that they had been friends since they were kids. It was kind of funny how they seemed to be such opposites, but they were friends.

I waited my turn and then stepped up to the counter and began to empty my pockets on the counter.

Eddie gave me a, "Good morning, Billy. How did you do last night?"

I told Eddie, "I think I had a pretty good night, but we will find out exactly after we settle up."

Eddie began to count the quarters in a very professional manner. He wrote down on a piece of paper the total of the quarters, the dimes, the nickels, and the pennies that I put on the counter.

Then Eddie counted the dollar bills. I had done my figuring before I left for the paper store, so I only had to put up enough money to cover the papers that I sold for the week, which was $16.62.

Much to my surprise Eddie looked up at me and said, "Hey, pretty good, Billy. You came out right this week."

A big smile came across my face. I felt pretty darn good for figuring things out like I did. It was not easy because I had more money than I usually got each week. The final total was correct: $72.36! I did feel rich, even if I had to give half to Ma, I still came out with $36.18 for myself.

I carefully took $36.18 and put it in the front left pocket of my jeans. This was Ma's cut.

I took the other $36.18 and put it in my front right pocket. This was my share. Now that I had things all sorted out, we could head over to F.W. Woolworth's (affectionately called the five and ten by us kids) and do my Christmas shopping.

Winchester Center was buzzing with activity this morning. All of the stores were open, and the last-minute shoppers were scurrying in all different directions. You could tell that it was Christmas Eve.

We made our way across Main Street to the hub of activity in the town square, F.W. Woolworth's. The front of the store was painted bright red, and all the windows were decorated with green wreaths. It really did look like Santa's workshop.

All of a sudden it came to me. Santa was in the Filenes store across the street. I might have to visit him before I headed home. I wanted to make sure that he got things right this year. We had a little trouble last year as I had asked for a new fishing rod and got a drop line instead. I also had to ask him if he had the same penmanship teacher as my mother, because his handwriting was just like Ma's.

Steve, Bobby, and I headed through the double doors in the middle of the building and immediately got overwhelmed by the wonderful smell of the roasted nuts that were in the glass case in the front of the store. There was a white cabinet with a glass box enclosure that had all different types of roasted nuts. There were peanuts, cashews, almonds, hazelnuts, and two kinds of pistachio nuts, white and red. I loved the white pistachio nuts because they were covered in salt. Before we left the store today I just might have to treat myself to some of those white pistachio nuts.

There were banners and signs hanging from the ceiling that advertised all of the items that were on sale. I felt a little confused as I did not know where to start.

I figure that I should get my bearings and come up with a game plan before I began. I walked aimlessly up and down each aisle. I was in my own little world when it finally registered that someone was calling my name.

"Billy Shields, are you here all by yourself?" I turned to look and saw Vera Vassali behind the cosmetic counter.

I smiled and give her a big wave.

"Yes, I'm here all by myself. I'm doing my Christmas shopping," I let Vera know.

She told me, "Say hello to your sister Ellen," and then she let me know, "my family will stop by to say hello to your grandfather and your family sometime tomorrow morning."

"Ellen told me this morning before I left home to say hello to you as well. I will say hello to Ellen for you when I get home," I told Vera as I headed back down the aisle.

Vera called to me, "If you need any help with your Christmas shopping, let me know."

I said thank you and smiled.

Bobby and Steve had gone off on their own to shop. They only had to pick up a couple of things. I had nine presents to buy. A present for each of my brothers and sisters, something for Ma and Daddy, and something for Aunty Sue, Aunty Laura, and Grandpa.

Then I realized that I did not have to buy anything for Tony because I was going to give him the tie that Mrs. Napoli gave to me. That cut my list down to eight gifts.

I stopped at the hardware section and decided to buy my father a new screwdriver, the kind that you can change the tip from slotted to Phillips head. It had an adjustable ratcheted handle as well. He did mention that sometimes he had to remove old screws and that they were hard to get out if they had been painted over. This new type of screwdriver should be helpful to him, and it only cost ninety-nine cents. One present down and seven more to go.

I got Ma, Aunty Sue, and Aunty Laura new aprons; they all matched so that when they were cooking in the kitchen together it would look like they were on the same cooking team. I decided to get a matching pot holder for Ma as an extra present because she was special and deserved something extra.

I got both Ellen and Gloria a pair of white bobby socks each, because they were always complaining that one or the other took each other's clean bobby socks.

For Grandpa I got him a box of Parodi Stogies. He loved smoking them. He could always use more cigars.

Now I was down to needing just one more present, Jackie's gift. This one had to be very special. Not that all of the other people weren't special, but I knew Jackie always bought the best gifts and he had already given me that beautiful "Flexible Flyer" sled, so I was going to make sure I got him something really good.

As I walked past the cosmetics counter I saw Vera Vassali helping a customer. I guess I was going to need some assistance on figuring out what to buy Jackie, so I'd wait for Vera to finish helping the person she was waiting on and then ask her for some help.

As I watched Vera help the customer and saw her energetic personality and her ever-present smile it reminded me of a story that my sister Ellen told me about Vera and what she did when they were little kids.

Apparently there was an old crabby lady that lived in the neighborhood when Ellen and Vera were little. Her name was Mrs. Gavoni. She was old and lived alone on Tremont Street near where Vera lived. I guess Mrs. Gavoni's husband had gotten killed in an accident at the Beggs and Cobb Tannery many years ago. She did not have any children and lived by herself.

As she lived alone and missed her husband, she had a tendency to be somewhat mean and crabby to all the kids in the neighborhood. If any of the kids went in her yard for any reason she would yell at them and tell their parents. She was always getting someone in trouble, and the one that got in the most trouble was Vera.

I could somewhat understand this because her little brother Charlie has had his share of problems and he got in trouble quite often himself.

The story goes that one morning while Vera was playing with a ball outside near Mrs. Gavoni's house, the ball bounced on the sidewalk and went into Mrs. Gavoni's yard. No sooner had Vera entered the yard to pick up the ball when Mrs. Gavoni let out a string of screams and numerous threats at poor little Vera. She actually scared Vera and made her cry.

Vera, being a tough little girl and having a mean and vengeful streak in her as well, decided to get even with old Mrs. Gavoni.

As one of her chores each day, Vera had to clean the chicken coop where her father raised the chickens that they got eggs from. Occasionally they ate one of the chickens for Sunday dinner.

The chickens would make a real mess by pooping all over the coop. Vera had to clean up the poop and throw it in a compost pile that her father had near the edge of his garden. He would use the mixture of chicken poop and compost to fertilize the garden.

Right after Mrs. Gavoni yelled at Vera and made her cry Vera went to clean the chicken coop. While doing her chores and feeling very upset about what had just happened Vera got this brainstorm of an idea. Vera decided to get even with Mrs. Gavoni.

Vera went into the house and got a cardboard box from the attic. She brought the box with her to the chicken coop. Vera proceeded to put all of the smelly, gross chicken poop into this cardboard box. Then Vera went back in the house, and without anyone seeing what she was doing, she found her mother's best gift wrapping paper along with a big red bow and a gift card.

Vera went back to the chicken coop and wrapped the box of chicken poop with the beautiful wrapping paper and then tied the big red colorful bow to the box. Vera then wrote in big letters on the card "from New York." Vera stepped back to admire her handiwork. Even though the box was filled with smelly, stinky chicken poop, it looked very attractive.

Vera waited until the coast was clear and then hid in the bushes next to Mrs. Gavoni's house. When the timing was right, she quickly dashed out of her hiding place in the bushes and put the beautifully wrapped gift box on the steps of Mrs. Gavoni's house, and she rang the doorbell.

The beautiful box with the gift tag reading "from New York" was sitting on the door step when Mrs. Gavoni came out to see who rang the bell. Vera was tucked away in her hiding place in the bushes when she saw Mrs. Gavoni break into a big huge smile as she picked up the box and expressed in her broken English, "Whosa senda me a this niza box froma New York?"

Mrs. Gavoni took the box into the house with her, and in about thirty seconds came back and flung open the door, yelling out loud to anyone who might be listening, "You no gooda sumina beetch a basted," and then threw the box into the street.

Vera got her revenge and had a great big laugh and a huge smile on her face for a very long time. The Vassali family strikes again!

I had been deep in thought when I heard my name again, "Billy, do you need something?" It was Vera, who had finished her transaction with the other customer.

I came back to my senses and apparently had a big smirk on my face because Vera asked me, "Is everything okay?"

I composed myself and in a very distinct manner asked Vera, "Can you please help me pick out a present for my brother Jackie?"

Vera asked me, "What do you have in mind? Are you thinking of something personal like some clothing or maybe a nice aftershave lotion?"

"The aftershave lotion sounds about right," I replied.

Vera took me to the men's section of the cosmetic counter and picked up a bottle of Old Spice aftershave lotion. She told me, "This is a very popular fragrance with young men."

She even opened a bottle and let me smell it. It really smelled good.

I told her, "I'll take it."

Vera told me, "It costs one dollar and ninety-nine cents, but I will give you a discount because it is Christmas Eve."

I really didn't think that F.W. Woolworth gave discounts on Christmas Eve, but I was dealing with a Vassali. They were known to make up their own rules.

Vera gift wrapped the aftershave lotion for me. She had quite a touch with the wrapping paper and bow. I could see how she tricked Mrs. Gavoni so well.

At this point I had finished my Christmas shopping. I had so many packages that Vera gave me a big F.W. Woolworth bag with a handle on it, so I could carry everything easier.

The grand total that I spent for Christmas gifts was ten dollars and fifty-four cents. This left me with twenty-five dollars and sixty-four cents. Not bad for a kid of ten years old. I would put most of the money in the bank and use the rest for bowling, or treating myself to a sub sandwich at Eddie's sub shop during next week, or for just having fun.

As a matter of fact, I was going to pick myself up ten cents worth of those white pistachio nuts as a treat to me!

While I was at the front of the store getting my white pistachio nuts I met Bobby and Steve, who looked at me with starry eyes as they saw me buying some pistachio nuts.

It was Christmas and I was in a generous mood, so I gave Bobby and Steve a few nuts.

We headed out of Woolworth's and crossed Main Street again. I asked Bobby and Steve, "Hey, you guys want to stop by Filenes to say hello to Santa?"

They both looked at me kind of funny and informed me that they had to get home. I sensed a little bit of sarcasm from the both of them when I mentioned Santa.

I knew what they meant because the jury was still out on Santa. I had heard the kids in school talk, and I knew that the whole Santa thing was in question, but there would always be in me the hunger for magic, for the supernatural, and childhood faith.

I had read the letter "Yes, Virginia, there is a Santa Claus," and I did believe what the writer told Virginia. I did not live in a fantasy world, and I was old enough to understand fact from fiction, but my faith in Christmas and what I had been taught in Sunday School led me to believe that there was a God above as he had already answered my prayers by having Jackie come home for Christmas this year. Saint Nicholas being real, well, we would just have to wait and find out.

We walked down Main Street and heard the Salvation Army band playing Christmas music. They were camped out in front of the Kennedy Butter and Egg store on Mount Vernon Street just around the corner. We made it a point to walk past the bell ringer, the trumpet, and the tuba player that stood next to the kettle that was hanging from a tripod. People would drop donations for the needy in the kettle as they walked past.

As we approached the kettle I found myself reaching into the front right pocket of my dungarees. I pulled out a dollar bill and walked over to the kettle and put it in. The bell ringer continued to ring his bell as he thanked me for my, as he put it, "generous contribution."

I guess for a little ten-year-old to put a buck in the kettle was something that the Salvation Army guy did not see very often. I did feel that we needed to give to the needy and to help those less fortunate. Those lessons that I learned in Sunday school kept coming through.

To get home, we decided to walk past the Christian Science Church on Mount Vernon Street and cut through Skilling's Path past the Saint Mary's campus and onto Nelson Street. This was kind of the back way home, but we were not in any hurry, and it avoided walking up Shore Road.

If we went home by Shore Road I would have to walk by Mrs. Napoli's house and with my luck she would pop out of the door and ask me how my new tie was.

The walk through Skilling's Path was awesome. As we walked, we could pick up the scent of someone nearby burning leaves. The smell of burning leaves was such an overwhelming aroma. It's kind of late in the year for burning leaves. There was snow on the ground. In October just about every Saturday afternoon the air would be filled with smoke from people burning leaves. Perhaps someone had a covered pile of leaves and decided to wait until we had a clear day to burn them.

We walked down Nelson Street and took a left onto Oak Street. When we got to the corner of Oak and Holland Streets Bobby and Steve took a right onto Holland Street and headed home. I wished them both Merry Christmas and told them, "I will most likely see you both sometime tomorrow to compare Christmas presents."

I continued down Oak Street and turned the corner onto Spruce Street and into our driveway. I was home at last after a very successful shopping trip.

When I walked through the back door and entered the kitchen I could smell Ma's tomato sauce cooking and the different types of fish being prepared for the feast. Ma and the aunts were busy preparing the feast.

Dad was at his usual spot at the head of the kitchen table reading the newspaper and listening to the radio.

I asked, "Where's Jackie?"

Ma told me, "He has gone to pick up Grandpa so that he can bring him to our house."

It was always a project picking up Grandpa because he had to put his leg on and make his way to the car, or as he called the car, "la machine."

I took my bag of Christmas presents and headed up to my room to wrap them. I had to use the wrapping paper that Ma had bought, although I would have liked to have used the fancy foil wrapping paper that Jackie's presents were wrapped in.

I did the best that I could with regard to wrapping the presents. After looking at them all wrapped and placed under the Christmas tree, it was clear to see that I was wrapping challenged. My presents did not look like any others under the tree.

I stepped back to admire the Christmas tree with all the presents underneath it. The tree did look beautiful with all the tinsel and the ornaments, but the best part of the tree was the lights. We had the old-fashioned lights that bubbled. They were all different colors and had these tubes that were a couple of inches long. The liquid in the tubes would bubble, and it looked like each one of the little tubes was boiling. We had been using these lights on our Christmas tree ever since I could remember.

Ellen and Gloria had trimmed the tree and did a pretty good job, if I do say so myself. Everything was falling into place for our Christmas Eve celebration. The fish were cooking, and the tree was trimmed. The presents were wrapped and under the tree. Now we just had to wait for everyone to show up.

I did not have any lunch, just a few pistachio nuts, so I asked Ma if I could have a little of her tomato sauce to dip some of Marino's fresh Italian bread into to hold me over until the feast was ready.

Ma put some piping hot tomato sauce in a bowl and cut me a couple of pieces of bread for dipping. What a great lunch.

I just sat there watching the hectic activities as Ma and the aunts were busy cooking and preparing what would soon be the best night of the year.

The Feast of the Seven Fishes

The Shields family was a fun-loving group that looked forward to every holiday, birthday party, and family celebration. However, the granddaddy of all celebrations was clearly the Christmas Eve "Feast of the Seven Fishes."

Ma's family, the DeLucas, had been carrying on the tradition of this feast since they came over from Italy at the turn of the century. Grandpa and Grammy settled in Winchester in 1898.

What made this tradition so special was the history that went along with it. Most Italian families would celebrate the Feast of the Seven Fishes or vigilia (which it is also called) while most American families would celebrate the occasion with some form of meat dish.

The Feast of the Seven Fishes has existed since ancient times. According to Grandpa, no one is really sure how it started, but the significance can be attributed to the number seven as being a very important number to Italians and to Catholics. The seven days of creation, the seven sacraments, and the Seven Hills of

Rome were just a few of the cultural significances that this feast had.

There are no set requirements as to what types of fish were to be served, as long as there were seven.

We first started with an antipasto that included olives and cheese and marinated vegetables. Along with the fish there was always some form of pasta dish and usually broccoli rabe, which is the Italian kind of broccoli.

Ma usually kept with tradition and served smelts, which are small, salmon-like fish that live in the occan but migrate to freshwater streams. The best ones are around three inches long. She took out the backbone and cleaned them. Then they were tossed in a flour and cornmeal mix and fried until they are golden brown.

The next fish would be baccalà, which is a salted and dried cod fish. This fish has to be boiled and served hot, almost like a stew.

The calamari is cleaned and cut into small pieces and served with hot tomato sauce.

The scungilli is a form of octopus and is kind of like a conch. It is best served with a marinated sauce, which is the way Ma prepared it.

She chopped up the quahogs and served them with a garlic-bread stuffing and topped them with seasoning and fresh parsley and then baked them in their shells. These are usually served with the antipasto as a starter.

The tomato sauce is made with the lobster in it. Ma would cook the lobster in the sauce and then take the lobster out, remove the shell, and then cut it up into small pieces and mix it in with the spaghetti and the tomato sauce so that you get spaghetti with tomato sauce and chucks of lobster.

The seventh and final fish, the eel, is regarded as a true delicacy. This is the main course of the meal. The eel has only one bone, which makes it easy to clean. Ma would take out the bone and then lay the fish open and sprinkle it with some seasoning and pecorino romano cheese. Then her secret cooking trick was to place a bay leaf on each piece of eel. She would broil these under the boiler until they have a golden hue to them.

It would take Ma and the aunts the better part of the day to put all of the meal together. Ma took great pride in keeping up the tradition of the seven fishes. I knew that everyone enjoyed the feast. However, this feast was very special to Grandpa because it reminded him of being back in Italy and being with his family on Christmas Eve.

Now that Grandpa had showed up at the house with Jackie we could begin the Christmas Eve feast. Ma and the aunts had outdone themselves this year. Everything looked, and I'm sure would taste, great.

Ma called everyone to the table, not that we really need an invitation; we are all anticipating this evening's feast. Dad sat at the head at one end of the table, and Grandpa sat at the other head of the table. I guess this would be a technicality as to which end was the actual head of the table. There is much pride and tradition in Italian families, and respect is very important. The seating at the table is never really assigned, but everyone knows where they belong.

Dad sat at one end of the table, Grandpa at the other, Ma next to Daddy on his right side, and Jackie next to Daddy on the left side. Ellen sat next to Ma, Gloria sat next to Ellen, and Aunty Sue sat next to Gloria just to Grandpa's right. Tony sat next to Jackie, I sat next to Tony, and Aunty Laura sat next to me, just to Grandpa's left. Now that we were all seated we could begin the feast.

Before we began to eat Dad said the grace and thank you. He was very sincere in his prayer and thanks. Dad recognized the fact that having all of our family together was a very special occasion. He especially noted the fact that Jackie was home with us this year and for this we thanked God, his son Jesus, and all the saints in heaven.

The antipasto was passed around, starting with Daddy at one end of the table, and the stuffed quahogs were passed around starting with Grandpa at the other end of the table. This procedure continued for each course we ate. It took us almost two hours to consume what took Ma and the aunts almost two days to make.

The food was fantastic. Each course was wonderful. We never rush through this feast; we always take our time and savor each course. Even the passing of the fresh Marino's bread and the companion butter was an event. I swear there was no other family that had the love affair with food that our clan seemed to have.

It was not just the food, although the food in itself was amazing; it was the conversation and sense of well being and the fact that God had been gracious enough to let our family partake of his bounty that made this feast so special.

Jackie talked about his adventures being in the navy and how special it was to fly jet planes. He talked about his buddies and fellow pilots and how all of the members of the squadron play a specific part in the making up of the flight group.

He told us, "When I get back to the naval air base I will be attending a briefing on some of the new weapons that have been developed and how effective they will be should they ever have to be used in time of war."

It was very interesting to listen to Jackie share his experiences and what he was involved with. He let us know how special it was for him to be home with the family this year.

It seemed like everyone had something to offer to the conversation while we were feasting on the seven fishes. Ellen talked about how New England Telephone and Telegraph would someday be offering phones that work by buttons, not a rotary dial. She said that she heard about this from one of the salespeople, but it would be quite a few years before they had the concept fully developed. We all had a hard time believing that you could call someone just by pushing some buttons.

Gloria told us how she had to deliver a meal at the hospital to one of the doctors that was working in the morgue and how she got to see a real dead person with a tag on his toe.

Ma got upset with Gloria and told her, "This is not the proper conversation to be having at the dinner table, especially at Christmas," she told Gloria. "The family of the dead person must be very sad. They will miss their loved one during Christmas. All of us should say a prayer for their family."

Gloria turned to me and whispered, "The dead guy must have been ninety-five years old," as she kind of chuckled.

Tony let us know, "The freshman basketball team is going to be playing Wakefield next week, and I will be starting at guard for that game." Tony continued to tell us, "I have been playing at the forward position, but the coach feels I have a good set shot from the outside range, so he is going to move me to guard to take advantage of my long shots."

Dad told us that both the aircraft carriers Wasp and Essex were in port for the holidays. He went on to tell us that both ships will eventually be put in dry dock for some major repairs. This was real good news because the navy yard had been slow, and there was more talk of layoffs, but now things would be busy for quite a while with both of these ships being overhauled.

Ma and the aunts chimed into the conversation between trips to the stove, the refrigerator, and the sink. It almost seemed like a production line the way one would clear empty plates and dishes from the table and the other would bring a new plate of food.

Grandpa just sat there sipping on his wine and taking it all in. He did love being together with the family. Every once in a while Grandpa would tell us about a story from the old country or in his broken English tell us a joke that he heard on one of his radio programs.

Grandpa did tell us, "I brought along my accordion, and I will play some songs after we open all the presents."

With Grandpa on the accordion and Ellen on the piano we would have a regular concert this evening. We seemed to enjoy music almost as much as we enjoyed food. Well, that might really not be true. Our love of food did exceed our love of music. But music was a close second.

We were just finishing up the last plate of eels. It had been a tremendous feast. We were all quite full, but we knew that after we opened the Christmas presents, we would gather again at the table for dessert and coffee. The night was just beginning.

Everyone assisted with the clean up of the rest of the dishes and joined in with helping Ma and the aunts to wash, dry, and put away the dishes pots and pans. There sure was a lot of cleaning up to do, but we all knew that we could not convene around the Christmas tree to open the presents until Ma and the aunts had finished cleaning up the first wave of food and dirty dishes.

At long last we all gathered in the den, where the Christmas tree was and all the presents were. It was almost time to begin the exchange of gifts.

To a ten-year-old kid, this was what Christmas was all about. Everyone found a spot and settled in. Everyone made sure that they had enough room in front of them to stack their bounty. There must have been at least one hundred gifts under the tree. They were all wrapped in bright-colored paper.

It is pretty easy to tell which present came from which person because we all kind of had our own type of wrapping paper. I guess we wrapped our present with the specific paper that we thought was the prettiest.

Jackie's were the ones with the fancy foil paper. The rest of the presents had plain old paper wrapping paper. Don't get me wrong; they all looked pretty in their own way. It was just that the foil wrapping paper stood out so much from the others.

Dad took his spot in the chair next to the tree; he was the official reader of the nametags and in his own comic style would announce who the present was for and who it was from. With Dad being the master of ceremony it was sure to be a comical and fun time. I think my father waited for this night as much as the rest of us did. He just did a better job of controlling his excitement.

With everyone seated and their bellies full of fish, the exchanging of gifts began I was lucky enough to be the official assistant to the master of ceremony. I got to pick a gift for Dad to read, and then I got to deliver the present to the person he announced. For many years I used to share this position with Tony, but since he started junior high school he thought that he was too big to be the assistant, so I got the job all to myself.

The first present I picked for Dad to read was one of Jackie's foil-wrapped presents. It was a small box about two inches square that was sitting right on top of all the other gifts.

I handed it to Dad, and he proudly announced in his very deep voice, "This beautiful gift with the fancy wrapping paper is for the queen of our family, the most beautiful and talented 'Annie Bananny.' And it is from our own special flyboy, Lieutenant John Anthony Shields."

My dad had many nicknames for my mother; he usually called her "Mim," but he also referred to her as "Annie Bananny" or "the Queen." Sometimes he called her his bride as well.

I promptly delivered the first gift to Ma. She had a big smile on her face and a look of anticipation as she slowly opened the gift. Geez, it always amazed me how slowly grown-ups open their presents. First they slowly removed the bow and tried to keep it intact so that it could be used again. Then they worked each corner of the gift to loosen the tape and slowly peel the scotch tape back keeping the wrapping paper from tearing as if it would be sent to the wrapping paper museum in Grand Rapids, Michigan!

Finally, she got the wrapping paper off; she admired the cardboard box that had Long's Jewelers written across the top of the box. She had this look of excitement on her face as she seemed to pick up the pace a little and took the top off of the cardboard box. Inside of the cardboard box there was another box; this box was a blue velvet box that had a gold rim running through the middle of it. By now Ma was literally beaming from ear to ear; she quickly opened the box (funny how anticipation speeds things up), and inside of this blue velvet box was an absolutely beautiful gold necklace with a big gold cross.

Ma took out the necklace and at this point had a smile as big as the moon on her face. She held the necklace up for everyone to see. As she held it up in the air she noticed that there was writing on the back of the cross.

She held the cross up closer so she could read what it said: "To Ma, Love Jackie."

Ma began to cry as she called Jackie over so she can give him a big hug. Jackie had a big smile on his face as he gave Ma a big hug and a kiss.

One down and ninety-nine to go; Oh my God, at this pace it would take until New Year's Day to open all of the presents!

The next present I picked from the pile of gifts was the special present I got for Tony, the re-gifted tie from Mrs. Napoli.

I put a smile on my face as I handed the present to Daddy, and he announced in his husky voice, "Ah, a gift to Tony from Brother Billy. I bet this is a special one."

I took the gift from Dad's hand and delivered it to Tony. He had a look of anticipation and concern on his face as he quickly tore off the wrapping paper. As Tony opened the box and saw the tie he started to frown (hmm, the same feeling I had when I opened the box). He took out the tie and held it up so that everyone could see it.

Ma was the first to comment, "Gee, Billy, that is a real pretty tie. You did an excellent job in picking it out."

Mothers are so nice they always say encouraging things to their kids even when they know they screwed up!

Tony reluctantly said thank you as he looked at the tie again and frowned some more.

I can't believe that I pulled that one off! That was a real coup. I did it; I got away with the re-gifting of the ugliest tie ever made!

Now that I got away with the biggest scam in the history of Shields family gift giving, I start to speed up the handing of the gifts to Dad and the delivery process. I had kind of a system working: as soon as the gift was delivered to the recipient and they began the unwrapping process, I immediately handed another present to my father.

I could tell that Dad was getting a little annoyed with my impatience, but he was on his best behavior. This being Christmas Eve and all, he was not saying anything to me.

There I was, ten years old and I had systems in place already. I was kind of proud of myself. I better enjoy the moment because the world could come crashing down around me at any moment. The life of a ten-year-old can be very precocious, and then again it can be very melancholy. I guess we had to take the good with the bad.

The rest of the gift giving was kind of ho hum. Most everyone got clothes. Geez, what a waste of money. Christmas was supposed to be about toys and fun things. But I guess as you get older you kind of appreciate whatever you get.

The only exciting gifts were the ones that Jackie gave to everyone. He gave Tony a combination record player and radio; it was an RCA Victor system. Tony was really excited to get this; so was I. I knew that when Tony was not around I would be using it too.

Jackie gave Gloria a brand new shiny Royal typewriter. She was ecstatic to get the new typewriter. Gloria was pretty studious, and this would help her with the papers she had to do for high school. She did not have a typewriter and really wanted one. My father had a gleam in his eye as well when he saw the typewriter he figured Gloria could now type his union stuff. He was involved with the Riggers Union in the navy yard and went to lots of meetings and stuff.

Jackie gave Ellen a new mink stole with her initials in it. Ellen thought it was the greatest gift ever. She was all happy and smiling and hugging Jackie. She held up the mink stole for everyone to see; she put it around her shoulders and modeled it for the family. Every few seconds she would open the stole and look at her initials in fancy white lace embroidered on the inside: ELS.

I kind of thought the mink stole looked like a couple of dead muskrats from the Aberjona River wrapped around her neck, but then again I was not known for my fashion expertise.

When it was my turn to get a present from Jackie, I got a beautiful new Zebco fishing rod and reel along with a tackle box filled with lures, hooks, bobbers, and just about anything you could think of that had to go with fishing. It was the best rod and reel I had ever seen.

I started to drift off in fantasy as I pictured myself laying into a huge pickerel or a giant hornpout at Judkin's Pond. Jackie knew how much I loved to go fishing. I would go to Judkin's Pond with Tony most nights in the summertime. We would show up at the pond just before sunset. We had our special spot at the trestle.

Jackie told Tony and me, "The trestle is the place where I used to fish with my buddies when we were growing up."

Tony wasn't the most pleasant guy to go fishing with because he made me do all the work: carry the worms, carry the tackle box, and do errands for him.

One chilly night in the early spring he made me go downtown to Randall's restaurant and get him a cup of hot chocolate. He had only one dime that he gave me, and I didn't have any money. I got him the hot chocolate and brought it back to him, and I then sat there and watched him drink the hot chocolate. Needless to say he would comment how it was the best hot chocolate he ever had and how much it warmed him up.

I guess doing errands and all the work was the price you paid for going fishing with your older brother. The truth be told, I really did not mind being Tony's prat boy. I did enjoy being with him. Pain in the neck that he could be, he was really a good brother, and he did look out for me.

Getting the new fishing rod made me think of the time last summer when Tony and I were fishing at the Judkin's Pond trestle, and we had not had much luck that night. It was getting late, and we figured we should be packing it in for the night. Then all of a sudden, Tony's fishing pole bent way over, and the reel started to chatter as the line began to run.

Tony had the drag set on light. Tony grabbed the rod and set the hook. My God, this was a big one. It was so big that Tony called me over to help him. Tony was standing on the edge of the shore when without warning the rod twisted and bent. The next thing I knew I saw Tony being pulled into the water.

Tony was not a big fan of the water, especially after his friend had drowned in almost the same place that we were fishing. At this point, Tony was into the water almost up to his hips. Fearful of the water or not, Tony was not about to let the big one go.

I immediately went into the water and grabbed Tony by the waist and began pulling him back toward the shore.

Miraculously I was able to pull Tony back to the shore. Tony was fighting the fish the whole time I was pulling him back to shore. Tony was getting tired, but so was the fish. At long last, with me holding on to Tony's waist, we were able to land the big fish. I say we because it truly was a combined effort. When he got it ashore, it was dark out and he held it up to look at it. What we saw we both could not believe. Tony had landed a huge eel that with no exaggeration was at least four and a half feet long and six inches around. Geez this thing was so big it could have swallowed small children.

Tony and I were so excited. It was as if we had just landed "Juddy" the Judkin's Pond monster. Women and children would now be safe again. Little dogs could again take drinks of water from the pond; "Juddy" was caught and no longer a threat to society!

After the excitement began to subside a little Tony and I packed up our gear (well, I packed up the gear as usual), and we immediately headed for Grandpa's house to show him our trophy. We knew how much Grandpa loved eels (cubathona as he called them) and how much he would enjoy eating this monster.

It was almost ten o'clock by the time we got to Grandpa's house. Yes, it was way past the time we were supposed to be home, but this was a special event. Grandpa was sitting in the living room smoking a Parodi Stogie, and the aunts were in the back room working on a puzzle when Tony and I burst into the house all excited about our triumph.

Grandpa had been dozing off when we entered; we no doubt surprised him and startled him a little with all of our commotion. The aunts heard us come in and immediately came out of the back room to see what all the fuss was about.

When Grandpa and the aunts laid eyes on the huge eel they could not believe that we caught it. Grandpa actually got out of his chair and with his cane made his way to the kitchen to see the big eel up close. It truly was a thing to behold. As was always the case with eels, they had lots of life in them, and this one was still alive and kicking.

Aunty Sue said, "Put it in the sink."

After setting the eel in the sink, the slimy creature flipped and flapped all around.

From out of nowhere, Aunty Sue drew back and tagged a giant slug with a cleaver to the head of the eel. Wham! She chopped off the head in one fell swoop.

My eyes popped open, and my mouth dropped in shock. Tony nearly fell backwards.

That monster continued flapping around the sink. Even without his head, he had life in him.

Aunty Sue stepped back and said, "Now that he is dead we can cut him up and put him in the refrigerator."

Aunty Sue, with great expertise, cut up the monster eel into six inch pieces and said, "We will have an eel feast tomorrow night. When you boys go home tell your mother to bring everyone over the house around six o'clock tomorrow night for an eel feast."

Grandpa patted Tony and me on the back and told us, "You gooda fishina boys."

Tony and I accepted our compliments with great pride and headed home. Although we got our butts chewed out a little by Ma for coming home so late, everyone was proud of us for catching such a big fish.

The fish story of catching the giant eel would live on and be told as the one that didn't get away.

I finally came back to reality and told Jackie, "Thanks for the great gift."

We had finally gotten to the last gift under the tree, which was another one of Jackie's special foil-wrapped presents, and it was for my dad. I had seen the name tag earlier and wanted to purposely leave it for last. Because I was the purveyor of the gifts I had the privilege of picking which gifts to give to my dad for him to announce.

I handed Dad the last gift, and he proudly announced, "This one is for me, and it's from Jackie." Like it was a real big surprise seeing that the only one that had foil-wrapped presents under the tree was Jackie.

Dad slowly peeled back the wrapping paper. Geez, the old man was becoming like the ladies with the peeling back of the wrapping paper. You would think with the way everyone handled Jackie's foil wrapping paper that it was made of gold not foil. Note to myself—make sure I pick up foil wrapping paper for next Christmas; it seems to have a magical effect on the recipients.

The old boy finally gets the foil wrapping paper off and revealed a shoe box. On the box was written "Bostonian Shoes, the finest footwear money can buy." Now it was a known fact that my father was a true aficionado of fine footwear. He had a semi-precious collection of his own. My father would often tell us that the sign of a distinguished gentleman was one that wears a good watch and a fine pair of shoes.

We were reminded frequently that we should keep our footwear in good condition. As Dad opened the shoe box he was surprised to see a beautiful pair of black Bostonian wing-tipped shoes.

The old man was really surprised. He knew that a pair of shoes like that would set him back at least a week's pay. He had some fine shoes, but he did not own a pair of Bostonians. The old boy was beaming from ear to ear with a huge smile. For my father this was an exceptional show of emotion; he did not get excited by many things in life, but a fine pair of shoes did seem to get a rise out of him.

Dad was truly thrilled with the Bostonian shoes he got from Jackie for Christmas. All and all, it was a great gift-giving session. Everyone was happy and cheery just like it was supposed to be on Christmas

Eve. Believe it or not it was almost ten o'clock by the time we finished opening the gifts. We all gathered our bounty of gifts and dispersed to put them away.

In a few minutes we were all together again in the kitchen. Ma put out the pastries and pies and put the coffee on.

Grandpa got his accordion out and started to play Italian Christmas songs. He told us they were Italian Christmas songs; they could have been anything, but we did not know any better. Well, at least I didn't know any better.

It had been a busy day, and I was fading fast. I got some great presents and was happy about how everyone liked what I gave them for Christmas gifts.

This was the time when my deepest doubts began to fester, I knew that it was Christmas Eve, and for oh so many years I would scurry up to bed with visions of sugar plums dancing in my head, hopeful that Santa would soon be on his way. Actually I never had a sugar plum, but the notion sounds interesting.

This year I kind of wondered if my run was over, if I had been visited by Santa for the last time. Only time would tell. I kissed everyone good night and thanked them again for all the wonderful gifts, and then I headed upstairs to bed.

I put my head on my pillow and immediately drifted off to sleep with what I'm sure were Santa's sleigh bells chiming in the distance as I dozed off to sleep.

Christmas Day

Christmas Day had to be the most exciting day ever for a kid. Although this was my tenth Christmas morning the feeling was the same as the very first Christmas morning I could remember.

On Christmas Eve, because of his wooden leg and how hard it was for him to get around Grandpa would sleep overnight at our house. Ma would make up the couch in the family room into a bed for him. Everyone usually stayed up late on Christmas Eve, and as Grandpa would be back at our house for Christmas Day, it was just easier for him to sleep overnight rather than go home with the aunts.

The first Christmas I really remember was the year that Grandpa had his leg removed because of the sugar diabetes. I must have gotten up at five in the morning that Christmas Day. When I woke up, I immediately woke Tony up so that he would come downstairs with me.

It was still dark outside when we got out of bed, but the Christmas tree was on and the lights were shining so Tony and I could see what Santa had left for us under the tree.

When I got to the bottom of the stairs and entered the family room I could not believe my eyes. Sitting right under the Christmas tree with a name tag that said "Billy" on it was an honest to goodness Rootie Kazootie drum set. I mean this drum set was the real deal; this drum set had a big bass drum with a picture of Rootie Kazootie in the middle of the bass drum. There was a snare drum and a cymbal on a stand. The bass drum had a foot pedal and all. This was without a doubt one of the greatest presents that a kid could ever get. After all, Rootie Kazootie was just about the coolest character that ever lived.

We had just gotten our first television set that year, and one of the few shows that were on the television on Saturday mornings was Rootie Kazootie. I could not believe how Santa knew that I liked Rootie Kazootie so much.

I did get a bunch of other presents from Santa and they were really nice, but the Rootie Kazootie drum set was just fantastic.

Although it was only five o'clock in the morning and good ole Grandpa was sleeping just a few feet away from my drum set, I just had to give the drum set a try.

I proceeded to beat on those drums as if I was Gene Kruppa! I mean, I was beating some real cool licks on that Rootie Kazootie drum set.

I had forgotten all about what time it was; I just wanted to wail on those drums. Not long after I started my drum solo, I heard Grandpa mumbling. I thought to myself, Oh my God, poor Grandpa is going to have a conniption fit, and I'm going to get my butt chewed out.

Grandpa had in fact woken up. He looked over at me and, with a smile on his face, gestured for me to keep playing. That had to be the coolest gesture ever made by a human being, especially one that was around eighty years old. I continued to wail on those drums. Grandpa just smiled and clapped for me. Now tell me Grandpa is not the greatest grandfather a kid could have.

Unfortunately the rest of the family was not as gracious and understanding as Grandpa. I could hear everyone from upstairs shout almost in unison, "Hey, Billy, what are you crazy? We are all trying to sleep here!"

I often wonder if Santa knew what the outcome was going to be when he left that drum set for me that Christmas. Perhaps he placed the drum set under the wrong tree? Maybe some kid that lived with a deaf family was supposed to get the drum set?

I awoke at around six in the morning. I guess the excitement of it being Christmas morning had me energized and awake early. It was just beginning to get light outside. I got out of bed and put my slippers on. I took a quick peek out of my bedroom window to see that although it had not snowed overnight, there was still plenty of snow on the ground to make it a beautiful white Christmas.

As soon as I came to my senses and realized that it really was Christmas morning that feeling comes over me again, that feeling of doubt and trepidation, that sinking feeling that Santa Claus just might not actually be. I blessed myself and wished Jesus a happy birthday and figured it was time to find out!

Deep down inside I really believed. In Sunday school I was taught the story of Saint Nicholas and how he was born in the city of Patara in Lycia in Asia Minor, which is now known as Turkey, and how Saint Nicholas came from a rich family.

The story goes that as a child he had everything that a kid could want. He was the only child in a very wealthy family. However, his parents died when he was young. He was well taken care of but had this ambition to do good for others.

Saint Nicholas became a priest and was loved by everyone, because he was so good to people. As a priest he wanted to visit the Holy Land and see where Christ was crucified.

Saint Nicholas boarded a ship to cross the Mediterranean Sea to Alexandria, Egypt, and would go from there overland to Jerusalem.

When his ship was halfway across the Mediterranean Sea a terrible storm arose. The sky darkened. Lightning flashed like swords in the sky. Great waves smashed against the ship. The ship began to break up. In one of the lightning flashes the captain saw Saint Nicholas kneeling in prayer on the deck of the ship.

The captain said to Saint Nicholas, "We are all past praying, Father; the ship is going to sink, so let me lash you to the mast and with any luck you might be saved."

Saint Nicholas replied calmly to the captain, "Nothing is ever past praying for."

As he said these words the sun came out, the wind stopped howling, and the angry seas became calm. The captain and crew were astonished at what happened.

The captain asked him again, "Priest, what is your name?"

"I am Nicholas," he answered.

Then the captain turned to his crew and said, "Remember that name, men. If ever we are in trouble while on the sea, call on Nicholas and he will save us."

The sailors remembered his name and told many others about their life-threatening episode that took place on the Mediterranean Sea. Nicholas became a legend and a patron saint to sailors around the world.

The legend of Saint Nicholas continues with the story of a poor nobleman that had three beautiful daughters. Each daughter was loved by a fine young man. But the poor nobleman could not provide dowries for his daughters, and without a dowry (a dowry is money set aside as a gift for the man that marries the daughter so that he can take care of her) in those days the daughters could not get married.

Three times, in the dark of night, Saint Nicholas threw purses filled with gold through the window of the nobleman's study. It was not until the last time when Saint Nicholas threw the gold into the nobleman's study that the nobleman found out it was Saint Nicholas that gave him the gold.

Saint Nicholas swore the man to secrecy. But such joyous secrets are rarely kept. The nobleman spread the word of Saint Nicholas's generosity throughout the land, and today everyone knows of the gifts that are given by Saint Nicholas on Christmas Eve.

At this point I recalled what Saint Nicholas had said to the ship's captain, "Nothing is ever past praying for," so I said a little prayer to Saint Nicholas and then headed downstairs.

I did not want to make the same mistake I made a couple of years ago with the Rootie Kazootie drum set incident. I made it a point to be cautious and not wake poor Grandpa up or scare him half to death, so although I was very excited and I made it to the bottom of the stairs in record-breaking time, I entered the family room quietly.

As it said in the poem "The Night before Christmas": "What to my wondering eyes should appear but…" This was the first thought that went through my head as I laid my eyes on what was the most beautiful thing a ten-year-old boy could ever see under the Christmas tree: a genuine, brand spanking new, unbelievably beautiful Schwinn twenty-six inch Black Phantom bicycle. This beauty had white wall tires, a streamline fender light, and an actual working tail light.

This baby had the special new four-wheel drum brakes as well. It had silver fenders over the front and back wheels, and the frame was black with red trim around the chain guard. The word Schwinn was printed in gold lettering across the black and chrome center section. But the most beautiful part of this spectacular present from Santa was that it had mounted on the front of the bike, a great big silver basket that was built especially for carrying newspapers. "Wow," was all I could say!

The Black Phantom had a big red ribbon and bow on the basket and a typed note that read, "To Billy, From Santa, Merry Christmas!"

My prayers had been answered! Saint Nicholas did come through for me. I was the happiest kid in the whole wide world!

I couldn't wait to get this baby outside and try it out. I had seen advertisements for the Black Phantom in magazines and even saw a real one when I went to Raymond's Department Store in Boston with my father last fall. But I never thought in a million years that I would ever actually own a Black Phantom. Wait until Bobby and Steve see this beauty.

It did not take long for the rest of the family to wake up and come downstairs to see what Billy got from Santa. Tony was the first one down the stairs. He saw the Black Phantom bike and had the same reaction I did. "Wow," was all that came out of Tony's mouth.

"That's a beauty," Tony said to me.

I could not believe it. The spirit of Christmas had even touched my brother. I could see that he was genuinely happy for me.

In minutes Jackie, Ellen, Gloria, my mother, and my father were standing in the family room wishing each other Merry Christmas. Everyone had a smile on their face as they watched me ogle over my new bike. By this time with all the commotion Grandpa was awake and enjoying all the festivities of Christmas morning in the Shields house.

Jackie asked me, "How do you like the Black Phantom?"

I could tell by the tone in his voice that he was almost as excited as I was to see this magnificent bicycle.

I told him, "This is the greatest present I have ever or will ever get for Christmas."

Jackie made it a point to tell me, "The newspaper basket will hold at least seventy-five newspapers, which gives you room for your paper route to grow. You won't have to lug the newspapers up Shore Road anymore; you will be able to get your route done really fast now."

At this point my mother informed us, "We should all start getting ready to go to seven o'clock Mass."

It was going to be a busy day, so she wanted us all to go to church early because we were all up already.

Everyone scattered, and I was left all alone in the family room with Grandpa. The Christmas tree lights twinkling as I took one more look at the most beautiful thing in the world: the Black Phantom. The light from the twinkling Christmas tree bulbs flashed off of the shiny paint on the Black Phantom, which made it look like it was actually glowing.

All of us except Grandpa were ready to leave for church by 6:45. Grandpa was exempt from going to church because of his wooden leg. We all wished Grandpa Merry Christmas and told him that we would say a prayer for him at Christmas Mass.

We took both Dad's and Jackie's cars to church. Tony and I rode with Jackie, and Ellen and Gloria rode with Ma and Daddy.

Saint Mary's church looked beautiful this Christmas morning with red and white poinsettia plants decorating the altar. All the candles on the altar were lit as well. It sure did make for a wonderful start to Christmas Day.

Monsignor Manion was the priest this morning. He gave a wonderful sermon on how we should get along with our neighbors all year long, rather than just during the Christmas season. Then he commented on how Saint Mary's Church was so full this morning and how it would be nice if the people that come to church on Christmas Day would come to church every Sunday.

I have to admit, we went to seven o'clock mass every Sunday morning. I did see a lot of new faces that I did not usually see on Sundays, but then again it was Christmas Day and maybe a lot of people had company visiting them for the holidays. After all, we had Jackie home with us, who was not usually with us every Sunday.

I went to communion and made it a point to thank God for all the good things he had done for me this Christmas season: for having Jackie home with us, for having Grandpa and our family together, and especially for the Black Phantom Schwinn bicycle. I was so excited that I closed my eyes and thought for a moment that I really was in heaven already!

When we got back to the house Ma got the coffee going. She was using the big coffee maker this morning because she expected lots of people to be dropping by today to say hello to Grandpa and wish everyone a Merry Christmas.

When we got home Grandpa was all spiffed up and sitting at the kitchen table ready to start the Christmas

Day celebration. This was one of Grandpa's favorite days of the year. Because he couldn't visit everyone's house because of his leg, all of the friends and relatives came to our house to pay tribute to him.

As one of the elders in the family the cousins always made it a point to say hello to Cosmo on Christmas Day.

Ma whipped up some scrambled eggs and sausages for breakfast (yes, the fat Italian kind of sausages that my Father likes) along with toast made from Marino's Italian bread. Ma also served baked beans. My father liked baked beans with his eggs and sausages. Yuk, baked beans for breakfast, gross!

All of us were sitting at the breakfast table and commenting on the gifts we had gotten for Christmas. I was especially happy because this was truly a banner year for me. My gifts started rolling in early this year with the flexible flyer sled that Jackie gave me at the Lincoln School sledding hill.

I also got the beautiful Zebco rod and reel and the tackle box from Jackie. Tony and I got an electric football game from Ma and Daddy; I got a model-making kit of a battle ship from Gloria; Ellen gave me a baseball bat, a genuine Louisville Slugger; Tony gave me a Hardy Boys book; and then I got a bunch of clothes from Ma and Daddy, and the aunts gave me a new winter coat.

I always got a new winter coat from the aunts at Christmas. They gave me other stuff too, but the winter coat was a must. Grandpa, who cannot go out and shop, would always wait until all the gifts had been given out, and then we would take out his wallet and call everyone over and give them a five dollar bill as a Christmas gift. That was always an excellent gift!

It is just after nine o'clock by the time we finished with breakfast. Everyone helped clean the table off because we would soon be receiving guests. Ma got out the nice coffee cups, saucers, and silverware along with the fancy creamer and sugar bowl and put them on the table with the pastries Jackie had gotten at Angie's Pastry Shop.

Dad got out the bottles of Anisette, Sambuca, and Amaretto and put them on the table with a bunch of little shot glasses.

When Tony and I were younger, the relatives would stop by and have a couple of shots of liquor and then give us a nickel or a dime and wish us Merry Christmas. We are too old now for them to be giving us money, but it was nice when they did.

Ma figured that most of the relatives would be going to nine o'clock mass and would then stop by for coffee after church. The first to show up were the aunts. Aunty Sue and Aunty Laura came in and wished everyone a Merry Christmas. Everyone gave the aunts a hug and a kiss.

Aunty Sue said to me, "Billy, a little birdie told me that Santa Claus brought you a new bicycle."

I was astonished that she knew about my Black Phantom.

I told her that he sure did as I took her to see the bike that was still under the Christmas tree.

She looked at it and smiled, and then told me, "Now, Billy, you have to take good care of the bicycle, and be very careful when you ride it."

I told her, "I sure will."

When we got back to the kitchen Aunty Sue frowned and asked Grandpa, "Have you eaten any of the pastries this morning?"

Grandpa grumbled and waved her off saying in Italian. "Stare quiete" which translated from Italian to English means keep quiet!

Aunty Sue was Grandpa's watch dog and made sure he kept to somewhat of a diet because of his sugar diabetes.

Ma chimed in with, "Suzie, leave him alone; it's Christmas Day."

Ma was kind of Grandpa's protector, not that he needed one, but Ma was the older sister who liked to flex her authority over her younger sisters sometimes.

Today was the day all of the DeLuca cousins showed up at the house. The DeLuca cousins were actually related to my grandmother, who passed away not long after I was born. Their father, whom we call "Uncle," was my grandmother's half-brother. They were a big family with a total of eleven children, four girls and seven boys. There was one set of twin boys in the group. All of them were married except the oldest daughter, who still lived with Aunty and Uncle a couple of houses away from Grandpa's house on Spruce Street.

Most of the cousins lived in the neighborhood. They were a very big family because most of the married cousins had kids. I always looked forward to the cousins showing up because most of their kids were the same age as Tony and I.

The next thing we knew, the backdoor opened and in walked both of the twin cousins with their wives and kids. It seemed like the start of a parade or something as they all traipsed into our kitchen. There were ten of them all together. Everyone was shouting "Merry Christmas" and hugging and kissing.

The twins were named Mario and Manny. And they really were identical twins. They looked alike and talked alike. It was funny to see them both together as it felt like you were looking in a mirror. Both Mario and Manny were about five feet eight inches tall and in pretty good shape. Neither one of them had any hair, and they both had a slight space between their front teeth.

The twins were very gregarious, as all of the cousins were. When they were around everyone seemed to laugh. Ma poured all of the adults coffee; Dad poured a shot of anisette for Mario and Manny. The wives just had coffee, and the kids had a glass of milk. They all tried one of the many pastries that were on the table. It really was a special day.

Mario and Manny talked in Italian to Grandpa, which he really enjoyed. The kids who ranged in age from nine to fourteen were all asking Jackie questions about flying jet planes and being in the navy. Jackie was very patient with them and answered all of their questions.

I took the two boys who were eleven and twelve into the family room to showed them my new Black Phantom bike. There really were all sorts of activities going on at 79 Oak Street on Christmas morning.

All of a sudden the backdoor opened and in walked another cousin. It was Salvatore and his wife, Ginny, and their two kids, Sammy and Betty. Salvatore had the nickname Sally. He was a little older than the twins, Mario and Manny. Sally was a great guy; he was a very happy-go-lucky person. Sally was a little taller than the twins and had more hair than the twins. Although Sally's hair was turning gray, unlike the twins who still had dark brown hair.

Sally wore glasses, and he always had a smile on his face. I guess he had lots to be happy about because he was a true war hero. He was in the army rangers and stormed the beach at Normandy on D-Day. He landed on Omaha Beach and got caught in a hail of bullets and mortar fire from the Germans. The story goes that he was one of the only men in his group that landed on the beach that day that survived the German onslaught.

Sally was awarded the Bronze Star and a Purple Heart because he took a bullet in the leg during the battle. He fought his way up the beach and single-handedly took out one of the German machinegun nests with a hand grenade. He was a war hero, but like most of the guys that fought in the Second World War, he did not talk much about it. He came back home and started a new life. Sally became a carpenter and worked building houses.

The morning just got crazier as time went by. The house was full of Christmas cheer as the cousins just kept coming and going all morning. This was an exceptional day for Ma. She really enjoyed entertaining and showing off her family. With Jackie home it made it extra special for Ma.

It had gotten so hectic in the house that I decided to go to the basement with Tony and play our new electric football game. Tony was the Cleveland Browns, and I was the New York Giants. We took Ma's egg timer downstairs with us so we could time each period that we played. It was as if we were the coaches of real football teams.

While Tony and I were playing the football game in the basement, Ma called down to us and let us know that the Vassali family was here. Tony and I scooted upstairs to say hello to them. Mr. Vassali used to work with Grandpa at the Beggs and Cobb Leather Tannery. Charlie was there along with his brothers and sisters. There were six of them all together. Charlie was the youngest, and his sister Vera was Ellen's age. One of his brothers was a police officer for the Winchester Police.

Mr. Vassali was a short, stocky man, but all of his children were kind of big. Charlie was almost thirteen, and he was already taller than his father.

Mr. Vassali also knew how to cut hair. He came by to see Grandpa every few weeks and gave him a haircut. Not that Grandpa had a lot of hair to cut. I think Mr. Vassali liked to come by and drink wine with Grandpa and talk about the old days. Mrs. Vassali was a relative of the Napoli family. It seemed like all of the people in the Village were tied to each other in some form or fashion.

Charlie was on his best behavior this morning because he was with his father, who I heard ruled with an iron fist. Charlie only acted up when he was away from his father.

He asked me, "How did you do for Christmas presents?"

I was kind of waiting for him to ask me so I could show him the Black Phantom. I said to him, "Come here and take a look at this." I was doing my best not to gloat too much, but the smile was hard to stifle.

I took him in the den, and I did not say anything. I just let him look at the bike.

Charlie's eyes flew wide open and with great animation he spit out, "Geezus, that's a real beauty!"

I let him know, "It's got a light that works, and the basket holds up to seventy-five papers, depending on the advertising." I could tell that Charlie was a little envious, but he was gracious enough to wish me good luck with the new bike.

The Vassali family only stayed for just a few minutes because they had a few more stops to make.

The house emptied out and things started to slow down as it got closer to noontime. Ma shifted gears and began getting things ready for our Christmas dinner. Actually she put the roast in the oven while the company was still there, and the tomato sauce had been simmering on the stove since the morning. Ma truly was a multi-tasker. She could entertain and cook at the same time. Ma told us that dinner would be ready at our usual one o'clock dinner time.

My father had this thing about dinner being served precisely at one o'clock. I remember when Jackie was in college, and Ma became very friendly with David

Grady's family, who were from Everett. Jackie and David would share rides back and forth to school as one weekend David's family would drive and the other weekend my father would drive. Ma would talk with Mrs. Grady on the telephone all the time, so they had become very good friends.

Ma decided to invite Mr. and Mrs. Grady over for Sunday dinner; this was a couple of years ago when Jackie was still in college. Ma made it a point to tell Mrs. Grady that dinner would be served at one o'clock.

Well, Ma had prepared one of her standard Sunday dinners that always started with macaroni. As I mentioned earlier one of the first things I learned in life was how long each different type of macaroni took to cook. I believe every little Italian kid gets this training early in life. I think this lesson is called Macaroni 101.

It was the Sunday that Mr. and Mrs. Grady were coming over for dinner, and it was twenty minutes of one. The water for the macaroni was on the stove and had just about come to a rolling boil. I knew that we were having rigatonis for dinner and my Macaroni 101 told me that rigatonis took twenty minutes to cook. If Ma put the rigatonis in now they would be ready at exactly one o'clock.

Apparently my father took the same Macaroni 101 course that I took as he said to my mother, "Annie, put the macaroni in to cook."

Ma, being the total diplomat that she is, replied to my father, "John, we should wait for the company to show up before we put the macaroni in, that way it will be al dente when we serve it."

My father then stated, “Annie, we invited them for one o’clock, so put the macaroni in now.”

Ma, being the dutiful wife, obeyed my father and put the macaroni in. Sure enough at exactly one o’clock the rigatonis were done. However, Mr. and Mrs. Grady were nowhere to be found. It seemed like we had a dilemma on our hands. Ma was beginning to fidget and get concerned because the guests were not here yet.

“Annie,” my father said, “serve the macaroni.”

My mother replied, “But, John, our guests are not here yet; how can we eat without them?”

My father stated, “We invited them for one o’clock. If they are not here, we will just have to eat without them.”

Like I said, my father had this thing about eating at precisely one o’clock on Sundays. So we sat down to dinner without our invited guests Mr. and Mrs. Grady. You could hear a pin drop as everyone sat down at the table and began to eat their rigatonis.

At about 1:15, Mr. and Mrs. Grady showed up. My mother was very gracious, yet somewhat embarrassed as she greeted Mr. and Mrs. Grady. She brought them into the kitchen were they saw that we had started to eat without them. They sat down, and my mother served them.

My father never looked up and never missed a stroke with the eating of his rigatoni. Needless to say the Gradys have not been invited back for Sunday dinner.

Sure enough at exactly one o'clock Ma announced, "Christmas dinner is served."

Dad was at his usual spot at the head of the table. The aunts helped Ma serve the macaroni to each person as everyone took their seat. Grandpa had not moved from the spot he had taken early in the morning except to go to the bathroom once.

With everyone seated Dad said grace, "Bless us, oh Lord, for these thy gifts which we are about to receive from thy bounty. Through Christ our Lord, amen." He added, "Thank you, Jesus, for such a wonderful day and for blessing us with such a special family and great friends."

Everyone blessed themselves, and then Ma added, "And thank you, Jesus, for bringing Jackie home to us safely for your birthday celebration."

Again we all said amen and then dug in.

Christmas dinner started with farfalle (they look like little bow ties) macaroni (twelve minutes; go ahead, try to stump me!). Then we had the usual meatballs and sausages that were in a bowl in the center of the table. They got passed around, starting with Grandpa.

The next course was a top of the round roast beef. Ma cooked the roast in a pan and surrounded the roast with cut-up roasted potato and vegetables such as celery, carrots, and onions. The roasted vegetables are cooked with the roast, so the top of the vegetables and potatoes are browned and the bottom of the potatoes and vegetables are soaked with the juices from the roast. A very delectable treat, I might add.

Ma served the roast in one platter and the vegetables in a separate bowl. The next course was Ma's famous salad. She made a simple salad with a mixture of iceberg and romaine lettuce, tomatoes, and cucumbers and just olive oil and wine vinegar dressing.

According to Grandpa, for Italians, salad is always served at the end of a meal as a way to cleanse the palate. The leafy lettuce and the vinegar help clean the mouth and take the heavy taste of meat from your mouth.

Christmas dinner was a leisurely dinner with lots of conversation. During dinner Jackie decided to make a big announcement to the family.

Jackie informed us, "When I went to the Fargo Building in South Boston the other day, I did in fact meet with my buddy David Grady, but I also met with Captain Martin, who confirmed that I was being transferred to Miramar Naval Air Station in San Diego, California, and I had to report there in eight days."

Jackie had mentioned this to my father a few days earlier but wanted to wait until the whole family was assembled before he made the announcement official.

This announcement came as kind of shock to the family. Ma started to get all flustered and choked up.

Jackie put everyone at ease as he explained, "I am being assigned to a new attack squadron that has just been formed. The squadron name is attack squadron VA-116, and I will be training for a world cruise on the aircraft carrier USS Hancock."

Jackie further explained, "I will leave San Diego sometime in the late spring of 1957 for the world cruise. This squadron will be involved with air shows throughout the Far East. We will be traveling to Hawaii, Singapore, Hong Kong, Japan, and many other countries."

Jackie was really excited about this opportunity. He loved to travel, and he loved to fly jet planes. How much better could it get for him?

Jackie then told us, "I will be driving back to Pensacola, Florida, to pick up my gear, and then I will head to San Diego California."

Dad told Jackie, "I am very happy for you and wish you good luck," as he shook hands with him. Dad also mentioned, "I am sure glad that you have a good car to travel in because you will be driving across the country in just a few days."

Jackie told us, "It will take me two and a half days to get back to Pensacola. I will spend a night at the base and pick up my gear, and then it will take me about three and a half days to drive to San Diego."

At this point Jackie dropped another bombshell on us as he told us, "I will have to leave tomorrow to start back to Florida. I want to get a jump on things and not go back after New Year's Day. There will be more traffic after the New Year holiday on the roads."

Ma again got all flustered as she blurted out, "You mean you won't be staying until New Year's?"

Jackie told us, "I am excited about this situation, and although I would love to spend more time with the family, I think it best if I leave tomorrow afternoon."

Things were moving a little fast for Grandpa, who did not quite get the gist of the conversation, but he knew it was something very important. Aunty Sue told Grandpa in Italian what was going on. Grandpa nodded his head and smiled and then patted Jackie on the back and shook his hand. There was a mixture of happiness and sadness at the dinner table. We were happy for Jackie that he got the new assignment, but we were all sad that he was leaving us so soon.

It was just about three o'clock, and Ma got up from the table and announced, "Dessert will be served later this afternoon around four o'clock."

Ma wanted to clean up the kitchen before the next feeding frenzy began.

As I said there were mixed emotions, but all in all we were happy for Jackie. He was very excited about going to Miramar Naval Air Station in San Diego, California.

Jackie shared with us, "I will be working on carrier landings. It is a little difficult to land a moving jet plane on the deck of a moving ship especially if the seas are rough. The ship is moving, and so is the plane, so you have to make sure your timing is right." He told us, "A good landing is when you hit the third wire. Although there are four wires strung across the deck of the aircraft carrier, hitting the three wire is what it's all about."

The kitchen table was cleared. Grandpa told Tony, "Go get the cards; it's now time to play penny ante poker."

This was a standard tradition of the Shields family on Christmas Day. Everyone had saved their pennies for the past few weeks so we could have our big card game. We played poker and bet with pennies. You had to ante up a penny to get your cards, and then you could bet up to two cents if you had a good hand. You didn't make a fortune playing this game, but we did have lots of laughs.

The funniest part of this game was keeping an eye on Grandpa, who had a tendency to . . . Well, how should I put this; Grandpa had a tendency to forget to put his money in, and then accuse everyone else of being what he calls "whosa shine" when the ante pot was not correct.

Grandpa was usually the one that did not put his penny in, but he always thought it was someone else who didn't put their penny in. This would be a fun afternoon.

We all took our places at the poker table, Jackie, Ellen, Tony, Gloria, Daddy, Grandpa, and me. Aunty Sue and Aunty Laura helped my mother with the dishes.

The card game was a million laughs. We were having so much fun with Grandpa. We were actually messing with him as sometimes we didn't put our penny in the ante pot, and sometimes we put extra pennies in just to goof with Grandpa.

Everyone was dealing their best digs to each other as the card game progressed. I swear Gloria had been writing down her digs all year and saving them up just for the Christmas card game.

Unfortunately I seemed to be the recipient of most everyone's digs! Instead of penny ante poker the game should have been called fun time with the Shields family as they picked on little "chicken bones." For once I really didn't mind because I was in such a good mood. After all I had the beautiful Black Phantom bike that I was going to take out for the inaugural spin a little later in the afternoon.

I called Steve and Bobby earlier and told them to come by around four o'clock before it gets dark so I could show them my magnificent Black Phantom.

After losing most of my pennies and getting picked on by just about everyone, I decide to call it quits. It was almost four o'clock, and I was itching to take a ride on my bike. I gave the few pennies I had left to Grandpa and then stuck my tongue out at everyone at the table and bid them farewell!

I wheeled my bike out of the family room and started to head outside.

However, before I could get past the kitchen I got the standard, "Billy, you be careful out there," from my mother. "There is snow on the sides of the roads, so you better be careful if you ride your new bike on the street."

I promised Ma, "I will be extra careful. I don't want anything to happen to my new bike."

I got outside, and sure enough, Steve and Bobby were just coming into the driveway. The look on both of their faces was priceless. As they looked at my Black Phantom their faces dropped. "Wow!" came out of both of their mouths at exactly the same time!

Steve shot a dig at me as he stated, "Hey, Billy, with that new rig you will now have to move to the West Side of town and ride your new wheels with the rich little lefty kids."

I was even taking digs from my buddies this afternoon. Oh well, the price you pay for fame and fortune.

I did get a chance to ride to the end of Oak Street where the dead end was. I wanted to stay out of traffic until I got the feel of this machine. It did take a little getting used to with the big basket on the front. I let Steve and Bobby have a spin. After all they were my buddies, so I liked to treat them nice even if they did give me guff every now and then.

It got dark really fast at that time of year, so we only had a few minutes to ride, but at least I got the inaugural spin in.

I let Bobby and Steve know, "I've got to go back in the house. My mom is about to serve the desserts."

Steve and Bobby waved good-bye as they headed back down Spruce Street toward Swanton Street.

I decided to put the bike in the garage. I didn't want to leave it outside because someone would most likely steal my bike the first day I owned it. I put it in the garage and put one of the old quilts that were in the garage over the top of my bike so if anyone looked in the window of the garage they wouldn't make out what it was. Hey, you couldn't be too careful when you owned a classic.

It was dark out by the time I got back to the house. When I entered the kitchen I saw that everyone was back at their assigned seats at the kitchen table feeding their faces again. Ma put out the pastries, and Aunty Sue made a ricotta pie. Aunty Sue made a mean ricotta pie. Aunty Sue used Grammy's recipe, the one that she brought over with her when she came from Italy.

There are two things that my family could do very well, enjoy food and talk. This had turned out to be a magnificent day. I was kind of sad that it was coming to an end. This would surely be a Christmas Day to remember!

The Farewell

It had been a long day for everyone in the Shields family; we all kind of crashed early on Christmas night. I was the first one off to bed as I had been drained of just about all my strength, with the early rising and the discovery of the Schwinn Black Phantom Santa Claus left for me under the Christmas tree.

It most definitely had been a great Christmas though. It could not have been any better. My faith in prayer had been reinforced. I'm sure Saint Nicholas had a hand in my good fortune. I did say a thank you prayer to Saint Nicholas as I drifted off to sleep.

I had the weirdest dream that seemed so real. It was summertime, and I was riding my new bike down to Winchester Center to pick up my newspapers for the afternoon paper route. I was riding on Shore Road just crossing the bridge where the Aberjona River empties into Judkin's pond when a fish jumped out of the water and landed in the basket on the front of my bike.

The fish began to talk to me as if it was a person. It was a large mouth bass, but it spoke just like a human being would talk. The fish was asking me what my name was. I was about to reply to him, when all of a sudden I woke up.

Now was that a weird dream or what? I wonder if the dream had some deep underlying meaning. Maybe the fish wanted to thank me and Tony for catching "Juddy" and saving all of the other fish from the monster eel?

I couldn't believe that I slept until almost eight o'clock. I guess I really was tired. Today would be a sad day because Jackie was leaving. I had enjoyed his being around for the past few days. It took a minute for me to wake up. When I did come to my senses, I figured I better get downstairs to see what was going on.

I quickly brushed my teeth and washed my face to get the sleep out of my eyes. I got dressed and put on my shoes and quickly bounded down the stairs. As I rounded the corner from the living room into the kitchen I was surprised to see everyone sitting at the kitchen table drinking coffee and chatting.

I said good morning to everyone, and then I asked, "Why is everyone home today? It is Monday morning, and everyone is supposed to be at work."

Ma informed me, "Jackie is leaving this afternoon, so I decided to take the day off so I can see him off safely. Daddy, Ellen, and Gloria were supposed to work today as well, but they are also taking the day off."

Tony let me know, "I don't have basketball practice today, and I don't have to work at the hardware store, so I will be around as well to see Jackie off."

Jackie gave me a big good morning smile and a wink. Then he said to me, "Come over here. I've got something for you."

I was a little curious because I didn't want any tricks played on me first thing in the morning.

Jackie could see that I was being a little tentative, so he said in his most sincere voice, "Come on over, Billy. No one's going to bite you."

I slowly proceeded, but when I got to where he was sitting, he handed me a little black book. I took it from him and wondered what it was.

Jackie explained to me what it was. "It's my daily missal that I have had since I was eleven years old."

I took the missal and opened the cover and sure enough, on the inside cover in cursive writing it said, "Jackie Shields 1944."

"Billy, I want you to have this and use it when you go to church," Jackie told me. "It has all of the parts of the mass in both English and Latin. It has the Stations of the Cross and all of the Holy Days outlined."

I said to him, "Why are you giving this to me?"

Jackie replied, "I have a new missal that I got for Christmas from Aunty Sue."

I said to him, "I don't remember you opening a gift that had a missal in it on Christmas Eve."

He told me, "Aunty Sue gave it to me when I was picking Grandpa up the other night."

I thanked him and give him a hug and a kiss, and then I ran back upstairs to put the missal on my bureau.

When I got back downstairs I sat down at the table and began to eat the piece of French toast that Ma made for me. I couldn't help but notice how everyone seemed so quiet as I ate.

Jackie told us, "I will be leaving right after lunch, so that I can get on the Merit Parkway in Connecticut before it gets dark."

Dad went through the route that Jackie would be taking back to Florida. Dad was familiar with the route to New York and knew a few short cuts to get to the George Washington Bridge in New York City.

A couple of years ago we went to New York to visit our cousins in Flushing Meadows, which is in Queens, New York. Ma's cousin Johnny Juliano was a mailman, and he had gotten hit by a car while he was delivering the mail. He was in pretty bad shape, so Ma wanted to go and visit him just in case he might not make it.

He did get better, which was good, but he had a bad limp because they operated on his leg a few times.

Jackie and Daddy were sitting at the kitchen table while Ma, Gloria, and Ellen cleaned up the kitchen. The phone rang. I answered it and heard Aunty Sue's voice on the other end of the phone. Aunty Sue wanted to talk to my mother. I handed the phone to Ma.

After a short conversation, Ma hung up the phone and announced, "Aunty Sue and Aunty Laura stayed home from work as well today to see Jackie off, and they want everyone to come down to their house for lunch with Jackie."

Ma kind of liked the idea that she did not have to prepare lunch today as she wanted to spend time with Jackie before he left for Florida.

The phone rang again. I picked it up, and it was Aunty Sue again.

She asked me, "Please bring me a couple of jars of your mother's blueberries from the cold closet downstairs. I'm going to make a dessert and could use some of her blueberries."

I jumped at the chance as I could put the jars in the basket of my new bike and ride it down to Aunty Sue's house. It was a little cold out, but I didn't care because I really wanted to take a ride on my new wheels.

I told Ma, "Aunty Sue wants me to go down to the cellar to the cold closet to get her two jars of blueberries, and then bring them down to her house."

Ma was not really listening to me. She was washing the dishes with this kind of glazed look on her face. I could see that Ma was concerned about Jackie leaving, so I figured I'd just leave her alone.

I ran down to the cold closet and walked inside. As I entered the cold closet I couldn't help but remember last summer on the Fourth of July when my father had gotten a nice big watermelon for the Fourth of July cookout. Dad had picked up the watermelon a couple of days before the fourth and decided to keep the watermelon in the cold closet until the Fourth of July.

This Fourth of July was kind of a sad day for me even though it is one of the best celebrations and feasts that the Shields family have each year.

A couple of months earlier at Easter I had been given a special gift by my sister Ellen. On Easter morning I received from Ellen a shoe box that contained six little chickadees. They were cute little yellow balls of fine feathers. They were so cute and cuddly. I named each one and fed them crumbs and water.

In a few days the little chickens got bigger. I had to use a bigger box to hold them. I went to Symmes Feed and Grain Store on Main Street and bought a bag of chicken feed to feed my little chickens.

Sure enough they got bigger and bigger, and by late April I asked my father if he would help me build a chicken coop in the backyard. Dad and I put together a makeshift chicken coop so I could keep my chickens. Every day I would feed them and water them. I loved playing with them. All of the chickens were roosters, so they did not lay any eggs.

The chickens were healthy and kept getting bigger. By late June the chickens had become big and noisy.

On the third of July my mother called me in the kitchen and told me, "Tomorrow is the Fourth of July, and we are having our annual cookout."

I told her, "I am looking forward to the day."

Then Ma told me, "Today is the day we have to kill the chickens, so I can prepare them for the cookout tomorrow."

A look of terror crossed my face. I replied, "But, Ma, they are my pets. I have been taking care of them since Easter; I love them very much."

Ma's reply was, "They are chickens; we eat chickens. We don't keep them as pets."

So without any further ado, Ma proceeded to the barn, picked up a small hatchet from Dad's work bench, set out a piece of wood on top of a crate, and made her execution platform. One by one Ma got the chickens out of the coop and chopped their heads off.

On the afternoon of the fourth of July as the coals were burning in the barbeque pit and the celebration was underway I was feeling sad but hungry. I decided to be helpful and bring the big watermelon that Dad had stored in the cold closet outside to the picnic area.

I went into the cold closet and attempted to pick the big watermelon up off of the second shelf that it was sitting on. When I got the watermelon lifted I suddenly realized that the watermelon was bigger than I had expected. Sure enough I dropped the watermelon and it shattered into a million little pieces all over the floor of the cold closet.

That little episode did not go over well. Here it was two o'clock on the afternoon of the Fourth of July with my best friend pet chickens cooking on the grill, and our watermelon was no more. It took a while for me to live that one down.

Needless to say I am very cautious as I pick up the two quarts of blueberries from the shelf of the cold closet this morning.

I hustled upstairs and told everyone, "I will be down at Aunty Sue's for the rest of the morning."

I figured that if everyone was going to be at Aunty Sue's for lunch, I might as well hang out there until everyone showed up.

I brought the two jars of blueberries with me out to the garage. I uncovered my speed machine and carefully placed the two jars in the basket of my bike. It was a little cold out, but it felt really good to be riding my bike.

Aunty Sue and Aunty Laura were busy preparing lunch as I walked through the front door of their house. Grandpa was sitting in his easy chair listening to the Italian radio programs. I did my standard greeting to Papa-Nona and to the aunts. And then gave Aunty Sue the two quarts of blueberries.

I kind of liked the idea of hanging out at the aunt's house for the morning. They had a Zenith television, and I could sit and watch while I nibble on some of those Schrafft's peppermint patties that the aunts always had in their house.

I was in luck, The Kukla, Fran, and Ollie Show was just beginning. There was not much to watch on television in the morning other than Arthur Godfrey so catching an episode of Kukla, Fran, and Ollie was great.

The aunts were cooking up a special meal for Jackie's going away dinner. I could smell the garlic frying in the pan with the chicken that Aunty Sue was so famous for. Aunty Sue made the best chicken cacciatore; there was something about the way she mingled the chicken with the peppers and onions and the tomato sauce and potatoes along with the oil, garlic, and seasonings that made it so mouth watering. I was looking forward to our going away feast.

As I watched Kukla, Fran, and Ollie I heard Aunty Sue call me to the kitchen.

Aunty Sue asked me, "Will you please go down to the cellar and bring me up some vinegar peppers from the ceramic crock. I need them for the meal I'm making."

She handed me a bowl and a fork and told me, "Get four peppers and put them in the bowl, and then cover the crock."

At the end of the growing season Aunty Sue took the peppers and green tomatoes that were left before the first frost and pickled them in a couple of big ceramic crocks.

I got down to the basement and got hit with the multitude of fragrances that were always lingering down there. There was the fragrance of the wine from over in the corner where Grandpa kept his wine, there was the scent of the vinegar from the ceramic crocks, and there was the earthy smell of the onions, cabbage, and potatoes that were kept in the root cellar under the bulkhead.

I noticed the pile of burlap bags and the old clothes and rags that Aunty Sue used to clean. She stored various items like the rags in the cellar. I saw the rags and remember last spring when Aunty Sue asked Tony and me to clean the cellar out for her.

It was close to the time of the annual ENKA fair that is held at the Winchester town hall parking lot each spring. The ENKA fair is a charity fundraiser for a group of ladies that help out the various organizations in Winchester like the little league and the hospital and a bunch of other groups. They had carnival rides like the tilt-a-whirl, the scrambler, and the Ferris wheel.

They also had games of chance where you threw the ball at the milk bottles and tried to win a doll and other kind of games. They had cotton candy and all that stuff that they have at carnivals. This event was the biggest thing to hit Winchester every spring, and it raised a lot of money for charity.

I would have to think that with the money that I had blown at the ENKA fair over the past couple of years that they could put a new wing on the Winchester hospital and name it after me.

Aunty Sue would give Tony and me money for cleaning the basement, which came in handy for the ENKA fair. Tony and I were cleaning out the basement, and we had to get rid of a lot of junk and rags and that type of stuff.

We decided to have Mr. Murphy, the junk man, pick up the rags and old newspapers so we could get some extra money. Mr. Murphy would pay you for the newspapers and the rags, so the little extra money we would pick up from Mr. Murphy was a plus.

As we were putting all the stuff together for Mr. Murphy to pick up I got this brilliant idea. Mr. Murphy pays by weight for the rags and newspapers. He gives you so much a pound for whatever they weigh. I figured if we cut out the middle of the newspapers and put a few full ones on the top and the bottom and where we cut out the middles put a few rocks in there and then tie them up with twine it would make the newspapers heavier and then they would be worth more money. I assumed that Mr. Murphy would never know.

I also got this idea to take some of the rags and wet them with the hose, so they weighed more and then stick the wet rags in the bottom of the burlap rag bag. With the extra weight we would get more money!

Tony was not too keen on the idea but decided to go along with me. We put rocks in the newspapers and dampened the rags. When Mr. Murphy showed up and weighed the newspapers and the rags, he gave us a funny look.

Then he blurted out in his heavy Irish brogue, "So you thought you could put one past me did ya' boys! Which one of you rascals put the water on the rags to make them heavier?" Mr. Murphy asked.

At this point, Tony had this look of fear and panic on his face. I swear he was close to throwing up. Tony immediately turned and pointed his finger right at me. It took Tony all of about three seconds to throw me under the bus.

Much to our surprise, Mr. Murphy put a big smile on his face and started to laugh. Then Mr. Murphy patted me on the head and said, "Hey, little fella, you are the smart one in the family; you'll go a long way in life."

Then Mr. Murphy reached in his pocket and took out a roll of cash and hands us four dollars.

Before he left Mr. Murphy said to us, "To get ahead in any business you have to be smart, but it's not a good thing to trick the people you are doing business with. Let this one be a lesson to you boys."

Mr. Murphy had been a friend of the family for many years. In addition to owning a junk business, Mr. Murphy was also the ice man that delivered ice to our house before we got our first refrigerator a few years ago. Our parents had known Mr. Murphy for many years.

Tony could not believe that Mr. Murphy did not tell Ma and Daddy what we did. We pulled it off, and we did not get in any trouble. I did learn a valuable lesson from that little business venture though. Honesty is the best policy!

I quickly ran upstairs with the bowl of vinegar peppers and handed them to Aunty Sue. I then went back to watch the end of Kukla, Fran and Ollie on the television. I loved watching those puppets argue with each other; they were really funny.

Aunty Laura called to me and asked, "Billy, do you want to do your favorite job?"

I replied, "Of course."

Since I was a little kid, when it was almost time to eat I would grate the Romano or Parmesan cheese fresh so that it had full flavor. Grated cheese should always be grated when you are going to use it not before because it will lose its flavor. This had been one of my jobs for a few years now. This is not an easy job. More than once I've grated part of my knuckles into the cheese bowl.

It was almost noontime, and everyone would be showing up soon for Jackie's going away dinner. I was sitting on the couch across from the fake fireplace that Aunty Sue and Aunty Laura had in the living room. It was really fashionable. It looked so much like a real fireplace with a mantle and a fireplace screen.

It had these fake wood logs that had a little light bulb type device that when you turned it on it rotated around and flickered to look like there really was a fire going in the fireplace. I decided to light the fireplace to give us a little ambiance on this cold winter day.

I was sitting and watching the fireplace flicker for a few minutes, which did have a kind of mesmerizing effect.

All of a sudden I heard Grandpa call me. "Hey, whalyo (kid), you litta the fire. Now itsa too hot ina here."

I started laughing to myself as I surely thought Grandpa was joking with me, but when I looked at him he was taking his sweater off and fanning his face with his hand as if it really had gotten hotter in the room. I shrugged my shoulders and went over to help Grandpa take his sweater off. The power of suggestion; you put on a fake fire and the mind thinks it's getting warmer.

As I was helping Grandpa disrobe the door opened, and I saw the whole family come through the door. They had arrived. Everyone gave the standard greeting along with hugs and kisses.

Jackie made it a point to give Aunty Sue and Aunty Laura a big hug and a kiss, and he told them, "Thank you for hosting this going away feast. I really appreciate it."

Jackie gave Grandpa a big hug and a kiss; Jackie saw the fake fire flickering and that Grandpa had taken his sweater off, which he seldom ever did.

Jackie said to Grandpa, "Caldo, caldo (hot)," and Jackie waved his hand as if he was fanning his face.

Grandpa waved his hand and said to Jackie in Italian, "The little boy made the fire, and now it's hot in here." Jackie had a big smile on his face and did everything he could not to burst into laughter.

Aunty Sue sang out in her somewhat insistent voice, "Everybody come to the kitchen; it's time to eat now."

We all sat down at the table and took our designated positions. Grandpa poured the wine. As he was about to pour Jackie a glass of wine, Jackie put his hand over the glass and let Grandpa know, "I'm going to be driving the la macchina (this is what Grandpa called a car), and I better not have any wine."

Grandpa looked puzzled but somewhat understood. Aunty Sue began to serve the food. We started with Aunty Sue's Italian chicken soup with pastena and chickory. Aunty Sue put some little meatballs in the soup as well. This soup was kind of like Italian Wedding Soup but better!

This soup was great with a little fresh grated cheese. All you could hear were spoons clanging against bowls and slurping noises. I guess with everyone being so quiet it was a compliment to Aunty Sue's soup. I also realized that Jackie would be leaving soon, and there were lots of mixed emotions going on.

The chicken cacciatore was served next. Aunty Sue had outdone herself this time. The big platter was put in the middle of the table. The aroma seemed to waft through the air, and then it attacked your nostrils like some kind of little Italian exotic dancer wiggling inside your nose.

The chicken was cooked to perfection, and the potatoes and vegetables were done just right. I did love that dish; it was one of my favorites, but what I liked even more than the chicken and the vegetables was the sauce that had been created from the mixture of the chicken, the vegetables, some tomatoes, the garlic, and the olive oil. This mixture made the best dipping sauce in the world.

I took a small piece of chicken and a whole lot of sauce. I dived into the basket of fresh Italian bread that was sitting on the corner of the table and tore off a piece of bread and "wooshed" it around in the sauce. Oh my God, it was like I'd died and gone to cacciatore heaven!

The conversation picked up, and the wine flowed. By the time we got to the salad everyone was in a good mood. Aunty Sue and Aunty Laura had done a great job preparing Jackie's going away feast.

I found myself sitting at the table and thinking of all the fun times we had this Christmas with Jackie being home. I smiled to myself, as I recalled the episode on Shore Road when Jackie pulled up behind me when I was carrying the newspapers that Wednesday afternoon and how he scared the living daylights out of me when he beeped the horn. Who could ever forget the grand entrance that Jackie made with Ma, when he escorted her into the Lincoln School auditorium on the night of the school pageant. Then there was the Flexible Flyer sled that Jackie gave me at the school yard.

The days that Jackie drove me around to do the paper route would always be very special. The trip into the North End and the policeman pulling Jackie over to give him a hard time about being from Florida and driving around Boston in the snow was a funny incident. Jackie telling us all the stories about flying jet planes and how he took the time to share his world with my friends and all of the cousins showed what a very special person he really was.

But I guess the greatest part of Jackie being home was how he made everyone so happy and how he seemed to spread Christmas cheer to whomever he came in contact with. We would miss him dearly and count the days until he returned home for his next vacation.

The blueberry buckle that Aunty Sue made for desert was really good. We finished the meal, and it was just a few minutes before two o'clock. Jackie announced, "I want to get started. I have a long ride ahead of me."

As a final toast my Father raised his glass of wine to the family and announced in his deep voice, "Many things in life may change us, but we start and end with family." He continued, "May God keep Jackie safe on his journey."

We slowly got up from the table and kind of awkwardly mingled and reluctantly shuffled toward the back room to retrieve our coats so that we could all go outside and say good-bye to Jackie. Even Grandpa made the journey outside to say good-bye.

Aunty Sue put together a bag of food for Jackie to take with him and eat if he got hungry while traveling.

Jackie said, "Thanks, Aunty Sue, for the food. I look forward to eating it later today."

Jackie walked around to the back of the car and put the bag in his trunk. Jackie's car was loaded with his tan leather suitcase and a bunch of boxes with gifts in them.

Ma had her camera with her and insisted that Jackie pose for pictures with her and with the aunts. Jackie, always the dutiful son, agreed with a smile and stood with the aunts for one picture and with Ma for another.

It was a beautiful day with the sun shining, a very good day to travel. Jackie, with the ever-present smile on his face said, "Good-bye, everyone. I had a fantastic time being home, and I will miss all of you very much."

Jackie then gave us all hugs and kisses. Ma started to cry, and we all felt sad. Jackie shook Dad's hand and gave him a hug as he opened the door to his Mercury Monterey. Jackie waved again to everyone as he got in the car and closed the door. That's it. He was on his way back to Florida and then on to California. We all waved as he headed down Spruce Street toward Shore Road.

It sure was great having Jackie home for Christmas. It was the best Christmas ever!

Epilogue

Having Jackie home for the Christmas of 1956 was a real treat for the Shields family. We had a chance to spend some very valuable time together. I know that Jackie enjoyed being home with our family just about as much as we enjoyed having him come home for Christmas.

It was sad as we waved good-bye to Jackie as he drove down Spruce Street. However, we understood that he had to leave to get back to what he loved to do most, and that was to fly jet planes.

Jackie loved being with his family; he had a great respect for all things that pertained to our close-knit clan. The connection that Jackie made with his family and his friends while he was home for the Christmas of 1956 will never be forgotten. Everyone in the family acquired a true understanding of what a very special and remarkable individual Lieutenant John A. Shields was and how fortunate we were to have him as part of our family.

It was a long drive back to Pensacola, Florida, for Jackie. He did make it to the Merit Parkway before it got dark. Actually he made it to Delaware before he stopped for the night. Jackie called Ma when he got settled in the hotel for the night. Ma was happy to hear his voice and know that he was okay. A mother always worries about her children, no matter what age they may be.

Jackie made it safely back to Pensacola, Florida, late the next day. He gathered his belongings and packed his duty bag with his uniforms and clothes. Jackie loaded the 1957 Mercury Monterey with all his gear and then said good-bye to the friends that he had made while he was stationed at Pensacola Naval Air Station.

Jackie was reflecting on the first day that he arrived at Pensacola as he recalled the history that was explained to him when he reported for duty.

When the United States purchased Florida from Spain in 1821, President John Quincy Adams and Secretary of the Navy Samuel Southard immediately realized how important the port of Pensacola, Florida, would be to national security. Construction began in 1826 and a naval installation has been present at this location ever since.

Pensacola NAS has been an intricate part of Southern history for many years. For Jackie, leaving this beloved place behind would not be so easy. The people he worked with and the civilians that lived in the area where very special people. Jackie remembered how he got teased when he first showed up at Pensacola because of his Boston accent. Jackie took it all in stride and never really got offended when he was referred to as a Yankee. He realized that it was all in good fun. Jackie had great respect for the traditions that many of the Southerners held near and dear to their hearts.

Jackie got on the road just before noon on Wednesday, December 28. It was not long before he entered Alabama and after a little while he stopped for dinner in Baton Rouge, Louisiana. Jackie had a quick bite to eat and continued on his way. As he drove he could not help but consider the fact that just a few days before he was dining on Ma's great food; now he was banished to crawfish stew and fried catfish. He kind of chuckled as he thought of the chasm between the Southern cuisine and Ma's home cooking. Jackie knew it would be a while before he tasted Ma's macaroni and meatballs again.

Jackie made it as far as Austin, Texas, where he stopped at a little roadside motel for the night. He felt a little cheated as he got into bed at almost eleven p.m. and was awake and in the shower at six a.m. Jackie thought he should have been charged by the hour and not the day for the use of the motel room, but the sheets where clean and the towels fresh, so it was worth it. After traveling for almost twelve hours and seven hundred miles it was time for a rest.

It was Thursday, December 29. Jackie had calculated that this leg of the journey would take about fifteen hours or so. He would be traveling almost nine hundred miles. The drive was long and boring; although he got the Mercury Monterey moving close to one hundred miles an hour during a long flat stretch through western Texas. One hundred miles per hour is pretty fast, but it was nothing like the neck-snapping speed of an F7U Cutlass.

Armadillos and oil rigs were about the only sites to see as he traveled through Texas. New Mexico was not a whole lot better with regard to site seeing. The terrain in New Mexico was not quite as flat as west Texas. Other than a couple of stops for gas and lunch, New Mexico was a blur.

Jackie pulled into Phoenix, Arizona, just before midnight and realized that he had pushed the envelope by staying on the road a little longer than he should have. He was tired and dusty from traveling through the desert and in need of a good night's sleep.

Jackie slept a little late because he did not have to far to go to get to Miramar Naval Air Station. It was Friday, December 29, and with a little less than four hundred miles to travel, Jackie figured he would be in San Diego by late in the afternoon.

When you spend almost three days on the road and travel over two thousand miles you have the opportunity to think and contemplate issues that are going on in your life. You have the chance to reflect on what has happened in your life thus far and what very well may lie in store for you in the future.

Jackie had many conversations with God while he was on his journey. Being a man of faith, he knew that it was always wise to include the big guy in your thoughts and plans. Jackie would consult with God on most of his decisions and strategies. When you fly jet planes for a living and travel at supersonic speeds, having God as your co-pilot is intelligent and sensible.

Jackie was very excited about the upcoming world cruise on the aircraft carrier USS Hancock. Traveling to the Far East and visiting such places as Hong Kong, the Philippines, Japan, and Singapore had only been a dream up until now.

Jackie was very thankful for the path his life had taken. Graduating college and enlisting in the United States Navy was truly a beneficial decision. With one more year left on his enlistment, Jackie was not sure what he would do when his hitch was up. He had not given much thought to life after the navy.

With a few more hours to travel Jackie gave some thought to the future. Should I continue as a naval aviator? How about becoming a commercial pilot for one of the big airlines like TWA or United? There were definitely choices and good ones at that. Being just twenty-three years old and having the experience of naval flight training and the command of a multi-million-dollar aircraft proved that responsibility was something that came natural to this young man from the Village. The future looked so bright for Jackie that he had to put his sunglasses on!

Miramar Naval Air Station is one of the largest facilities on the west coast. The base encompasses a total of 24,000 acres and was the home of attack fighter squadron VA-116.

As Jackie rolled up to the guard post and flashed his credentials, the marine on duty gave Jackie a salute and waved him through. First impressions are lasting impressions. The size of this facility was much bigger than Pensacola, Florida, or Corpus Christie, Texas, where he had been stationed previously.

Jackie knew that this place will be home for now, so he better get the lay of the land and find his way around this place and make the best of the situation.

Jackie checked in with his commanding officer, letting him know that he had arrived. The commanding officer, Captain Jenks, let Jackie know that he was happy to have him as part of the team and that he was looking forward to flying with the group once everyone was assembled.

Jackie found his quarters, with the help of an enlisted man, and he began to unpack and store his gear. Tomorrow would be orientation and briefing day and then with any luck it would be up in the air in a day or so.

Jackie was up and out of his room before 0600 hours and in the officer's mess hall when he saw his commanding officer. The commanding officer, Captain Jenks, grabbed some chow and headed over to where Jackie was sitting and joined him.

"How did you sleep your first night at Miramar?" Captain Jenks asked Jackie.

"Very well, sir, thank you," Jackie replied.

"Are you ready for a full day of orientation and briefing?" Captain Jenks asked Jackie.

"Yes, sir, I'm looking forward to it," Jackie replied.

Jackie, was cool as ever, found himself in a conversation with the commanding officer on his first morning at the base. Jackie figured that the commanding officer was trying to size up his new pilot and get to know him a little better.

It did not take long until Jackie and the commanding officer were joined at their table by a couple more of the new pilots. They all shook hands and introduced themselves and gave a short introduction as to where they were from and what they had been doing before joining each other at Miramar.

They finished breakfast and headed over to the briefing room and settled in for a full day of seminars and orientation as they all got acquainted with their new squadron VA-116.

After a full day of orientation and another day of logistics and weapons training the squadron was ready to take to the air. Their first hop would be a night flight and would take them up to Los Angeles and then back to San Diego.

There was a little anticipation and a lot of excitement as the pilots took their places in their designated aircraft. With an ear-piercing roar each jet took to the air one by one. Once they were airborne they fly in formation up the coast of California.

For Jackie, flying over Los Angeles at night was breath-taking. All of the bright lights and buildings made it seem as if you were looking down from heaven. Jackie considered himself one of the luckiest people on earth to be flying a jet plane at night over Los Angeles. He wished that everyone in the world could have this experience.

They got back to Miramar at 2300 hours and then sat in for a debriefing that took until midnight. With his first hop at Miramar under his belt, Jackie was feeling energized and alive. Jackie got back to his quarters and he decided to write a few letters as he was not quite ready for the sack just yet.

Jackie opened the desk drawer in his room and found a stack of writing paper with the VA-116 emblem on the stationary letterhead. With a smile on his face he put pen to paper and proceeded to drop all of us a quick note. Jackie started each letter by telling us how much he enjoyed being home for Christmas and how he made it safely to San Diego. Jackie was very good at writing letters, especially to Ma. He wrote her at least once a week.

Jackie had many excellent qualities. In addition to being a cracker jack pilot, he had very good people skills as well. It was amazing how when you were with him you felt relaxed and at ease. Jackie always made you feel comfortable and important when he had a conversation with you. Some people are given special gifts in life.

After a couple of days Jackie had settled into his new home and developed a bond with his fellow pilots. The warm Southern California climate seemed to suit Jackie well. He was working hard and learning new weapon delivery systems and flying tactics. On weekends the squadron would participate in air shows at different locations on the West Coast. The squadron was training hard for their upcoming world cruise and looking forward to performing air shows in the Far East.

Everything was going fine except for one problem. The F7U Cutlass that the VA-116 squadron flew was designed with a split tail and was a very maneuverable airplane, but this particular aircraft had more than its share of mechanical problems.

Jackie would let us know in the letters that he sent home that very seldom were all of the F7U Cutlass airplanes on the flight line. There were planes being taken out of service for repairs and alterations more frequently than the pilots wanted them. Safety was paramount, so the pilots understood the need to make things right with each plane. The fact that there had been some close calls with landing gear collapsing and flame outs of the engines was cause for concern for Jackie and his fellow pilots. Jackie let us know that it was an honor to fly with the VA-116 squadron and that he admired his pilot colleagues very much.

Jackie sent Ma a letter dated January 26, 1957, and he let her know that he was going to be speaking to about one hundred boys at a Boy Scout meeting in a couple of days. Jackie would be explaining to them what it's like flying jet planes and what it is like being a Naval Aviator. Jackie loved working with kids. I knew personally how much he enjoyed taking the time to explain things to young people and to enlighten them as to how an officer and a gentleman conducts himself while in the United States Navy.

On Saturday afternoon February 2, 1957, while on a routine training flight, Jackie began to experience trouble with his aircraft. The problems started as soon as he got off the ground. The area where the plane got into trouble was directly above a marine corps firing range that was adjacent to the base.

According to the eyewitnesses that observed the situation, the F7U Cutlass caught fire immediately after takeoff. Jackie got the plane to climb, but it began to barrel roll toward the ground. Jackie tried valiantly to save the plane but it was totally engulfed in flames. With the plane on fire and falling fast, Jackie ejected from the aircraft, but because he was so close to the ground when he bailed out, his parachute never opened. Jackie was killed instantly upon impact with the ground.

Jackie was twenty-three years old when he died while in the service of the country that he loved so much. February 2, 1957, was, and always would be, a tragic day for the Shields family.

It was Sunday morning, February 3, 1957. I was home with a winter cold and sitting around reading the funny pages when my brother Tony came running into the house crying. Tony had been visiting Grandpa and the aunts and was coming home when he saw a strange man standing in front of the house on the Oak Street Side. Tony asked the man what he was doing there. The man let Tony know that he was with Western Union and that he had to deliver a telegram to the home of Lieutenant John Anthony

Shields. The man asked Tony if this was the home of Lieutenant John Anthony Shields.

As soon as the man told Tony who he was and what he had to do, Tony put two and two together and realized that something bad must have happened to Jackie. Tony left the man and ran into the house, crying and yelling that something happened to Jackie. Ma, Daddy, Ellen, Gloria, and I were all staring at Tony and trying to make out what he was saying when the front doorbell rang. All of us bolted to the door together. Daddy opened the door. Ma had begun to cry already. The Western Union man was standing at the door, and he was crying as well.

With tears flowing down his cheeks, the Western Union man asked my father, "Is this the home of Lieutenant John Anthony Shields?"

My father answered with a quivering voice, "Yes this is his home."

The Western Union man then asked, "Are you John J. Shields."

Again my father answered, "Yes, I am John J. Shields."

The Western Union man handed my father the telegram and then asked him to sign for it. My father quickly opened the telegram while all of us were looking over his shoulder. Upon opening the telegram my father turned with a blank expression on his face and announced, "Jackie has been killed in a plane crash."

The words that my father spoke cut through me like a knife. I remember the wind being sucked from my body as the words that he spoke sank into my brain.

My mother, at this point, had collapsed and was sitting on the couch shaking like a leaf and rocking back and forth with her hands on her face just chanting, "Jackie, Jackie, oh my darling son Jackie, what have they done to you?"

All of us where crying and in shock. We never thought this day would come. However, we all knew that we had to accept reality and understand that when you fly jet planes for a living life can be dangerous and accidents can happen.

I remember Gloria hugging me as we both cried in each other's arms. Ellen was hugging Tony, and Daddy was trying to console Ma. The situation was about as sad as you could imagine.

It was not long after the Western Union man had delivered the telegram that the front doorbell rang again. This time it was two naval officers who were dispatched from the Fargo Building in Boston to explain things to us and try to comfort our family.

With the family in turmoil Ellen was smart enough to contact Aunty Sue and Aunty Laura so that they could join our family and be with their sister in her time of need. It did not take long for bad news to travel, especially in the Village. Within a few minutes the neighborhood was aware of the tragedy as they began stopping by to pay their respects to my parents. By early afternoon John and Gene Lane, the brothers that owned Lane Funeral Home, were at the house and doing what they could to help and console.

Aunty Sue and Aunty Laura drove to the house and brought Grandpa with them so that he could share in our grieving.

I will never forget Grandpa sitting in a chair in the kitchen and saying in his broken English, while he cried out loud, "Why didn't you take me, God? I'm an old man; why did you take the young one?"

To say that our home was like a crazy house would be an understatement. Doctor Shehan had to be called to take a look at Ma, because she had been screaming crying non-stop for a couple of hours.

Tony and I just stayed out of everyone's way; we both figured that Mom and Dad had enough headaches that they should not have to keep an eye on us. Tony and I got out the photo albums and just thumbed through the pages looking at pictures of Jackie but not saying anything to each other.

It had been a long and sorrowful day, but the grieving had just begun. On Monday morning the house had quieted down some, but Ma was still sniffling and crying. Everyone stayed home from work and school so that we could be together.

As you age you understand that death is a part of life. Whether the death comes suddenly, comes unexpectedly or takes place over time, experiencing the death of someone you love is never easy. Grieving hurts!

I have often wondered why God let bad things happen to good people. However, I also understand that as it states in The Lord's Prayer "thy will be done on earth as it is in heaven." The hardest thing we have to accept in life is God's will.

As a boy of ten years old I had my own simplistic way of dealing with and understanding Jackie's death. Now bear with me as this is kind of obscure, but it sure did help me deal with the tragedy.

In my childish mind I had this great vision of a major battle being waged between God and the devil. It was a horrific battle and God's troops were on the verge of being defeated. This is when God proclaimed that the only way that he could beat the devil was to enlist the services of a warrior that had proven his ability to do good and be worthy of denying the temptation of the devil.

God looked far and wide for the right person to lead his troops into battle. After searching the entire earth he decided that the only person to guide his forces, which would allow God the opportunity to beat the devil, would be Lieutenant John Anthony Shields. In my heart I know that Jackie was called to heaven for a very good reason.

On Tuesday my parents received another Western Union telegram. This telegram came from the Department of the Navy and informed my Father that there would be a military service and a high mass at Miramar Naval Air Station and then the remains would be shipped to Logan Airport in Boston. The telegram asked that the funeral people meet the plane and transport the remains to the Lane Funeral Home in Winchester.

On Saturday February 9, 1957, on a cloudy, cold, and windy day the funeral of Lieutenant John Anthony Shields took place. I was just a kid of ten years old, but I remember the day as if it were yesterday. Jackie had a beautiful funeral; if you are allowed to call funerals beautiful. He was afforded full military honors.

I remember the pall bearers in their full dress uniforms with white hats and white gloves. As the casket was placed on the grave pedestal, the pall bearers removed their white gloves and placed them on top of the casket. I remember how the flag that had draped the casket was folded so carefully and how the pall bearer handed the flag to my mother and then saluted her. I remember how startled I was when they fired the guns and how I jumped because I was scared. However the memory that remains with me the most is the eerie sound of the bugle as taps was played.

Ma never got over the death of her first born. For that matter, neither did my father. They both had sadness in their hearts until the day they joined Jackie in heaven.

Ma would walk up Shore Road after work, and there was never a day that by the time she got to seventy-nine Oak Street that she did not have tears in her eyes.

Grandpa passed away on Thanksgiving Day in 1958. As best we could tell he was about eighty-two years old. Grandpa was kind of funny about his birth date. No one ever really knew when his birthday was. Just to keep things legal, we would have two birthday parties a year for Grandpa: one in the summer and one in the winter. I think he kept his birth date a secret because he enjoyed the parties so much.

Dad passed away on November 18, 1980, just a few days after his seventy-second birthday. Ma passed away a year and a half later in June of 1982. She was seventy-six years old.

Aunty Sue died in May of 2000. She was ninety-four years old, and Aunty Laura died in March of 2010. She was a couple of months shy of her one hundred and second birthday.

Ellen got married in November of 1958, just a couple of weeks before Grandpa died. She lives on Cape Cod with her husband, Ralph. They have four children and seven grandchildren. Gloria got married in August of 1959 and lives in Charleston, South Carolina, with her husband, Bob. Gloria has three children and five grandchildren.

Tony got married in 1968 and lives in Billerica, Massachusetts, with his wife Lois. He has three children and two grandchildren.

I got married in 1973 and live in Middleton, Massachusetts, with my wife, Maria. We have three children and one grandchild. My office is still in Winchester; we lived in Winchester until I was almost sixty years old.

The Christmas of 1956 was a magical time that will always be remembered. It was the last time the Shields family was together for a Christmas celebration.

I wrote this memoir in honor of my brother Jackie, who I think of and pray for every single day of my life. I will never forget Jackie and the wonderful time that we spent together those few days that he was home in 1956 when the Shields family enjoyed The Farewell Christmas.